ENJOYING THE GOOD LIFE
STUART BRISCOE

D0097447

T2 CUN 645

While this book is intended for the reader's personal enjoyment and profit, it is also designed for group study. A leader's guide with Reproducible Response Sheets is available from your bookstore or from the publisher.

VICTOR BOOKS®
A DIVISION OF SCRIPTURE PRESS PUBLICATIONS INC.
USA CANADA ENGLAND

Copyediting: Carole Streeter and Barbara Williams

Cover Design: Larry Taylor

Library of Congress Cataloging-in-Publication Data

Briscoe, D. Stuart
    Enjoying the good life / Stuart Briscoe.
      p.   cm.
    ISBN 0-89693-960-X
    1. Bible. O.T. Deuteronomy—Criticism, interpretation, etc.
2. Bible. O.T. Deuteronomy—Study and teaching. 3. Christian
life—Biblical teaching. I. Title.
    BS1275.2.B75 1992
    222'.1506—dc20

                                       91-36932
                                         CIP

CONTENTS

With grateful thanks . . .

To the congregation of Elmbrook Church to whom these thoughts were first presented

To my secretary, Georgia Douglass, by whom the manuscript was prepared

To Carole Streeter because of whom the manuscript became slightly more understandable

To Jill, my wife, with whom for more than thirty years I have enjoyed the good life.

These are the words Moses spoke to all Israel in the desert east of the Jordan — that is, in the Arabah — opposite Suph, between Paran and Tophel, Laban, Hazeroth and Dizahab. (It takes eleven days to go from Horeb to Kadesh Barnea by the Mount Seir road.)

"In the fortieth year, on the first day of the eleventh month, Moses proclaimed to the Israelites all that the Lord had commanded him concerning them. This was after he had defeated Sihon king of the Amorites, who reigned in Heshbon, and at Edrei had defeated Og king of Bashan, who reigned in Ashtaroth.

"East of the Jordan in the territory of Moab, Moses began to expound this law, saying:

"The Lord our God said to us at Horeb, 'You have stayed long enough at this mountain. Break camp and advance into the hill country of the Amorites; go to all the neighboring peoples in the Arabah, in the mountains, in the western foothills, in the Negev, and along the coast, to the land of the Canaanites and to Lebanon, as far as the great river, the Euphrates. See, I have given you this land. Go in and take possession of the land that the Lord swore He would give to your fathers — to Abraham, Isaac, and Jacob — and to their descendants after them.' "

Deuteronomy 1:1-8

THE GOOD LIFE IN THE LAND OF PROMISE

1 "In the fortieth year, on the first day of the eleventh month, Moses proclaimed to the Israelites all that the Lord had commanded him concerning them. This was after he had defeated Sihon king of the Amorites, who reigned in Heshbon, and at Edrei had defeated Og king of Bashan, who reigned in Ashtaroth. East of the Jordan in the territory of Moab, Moses began to expound this law" (Deuteronomy 1:3-5).

Moses was addressing the Children of Israel immediately prior to their entering the Promised Land. He described the land as full of "all kinds of good things" that God intended for them to enjoy. (See Deuteronomy 6.) He also insisted that the people should do what was right and good.

When I put all that together, I realized that Moses was talking about "enjoying the good life." As I have watched people in many parts of the world, I have discovered that "enjoying the good life" is what they are most interested in. And it occurred to me that a study of the Book of Deuteronomy would give some insight into God's views on "enjoying the good life." You will not be surprised to know that they are somewhat different from popular opinion!

9

One of the concerns of politicians is what they call the "distribution of wealth." The idea is that a society has a certain total financial value and the members of that society ought to share in that value. Accordingly, the political debate is about how is this wealth to be distributed. My understanding of the liberal position is that because too much wealth finds its way into too few hands, taxation, regulation, and federal subsidies should be introduced to make income distribution more equitable. Conservatives, however, believe that business, freed of regulations and taxes, will produce wealth which will be reinvested in order to create new jobs. This will increase production, stimulate consumer demand and, in turn, generate more profits and even more jobs. And so, everyone will enjoy a bigger piece of the pie. The liberals suggest that the distribution of wealth will be brought about by government involvement, and conservatives insist that the government get out of the action. It is obvious that these two basic political philosophies are poles apart; and yet they raise a similar question: how can people acquire the means to enable them to enjoy the good life?

Unfortunately, we don't all think too deeply about these things, and politicians aren't always helpful in this regard. They say things like, "The liberal approach is tax and tax, spend and spend." To which the liberals respond, "The conservatives want the rich to get richer and the poor to get poorer." Conservatives insist that the liberal approach is to strengthen the weak by weakening the strong and to help the poor by destroying the rich, adding that liberals will not solve anything unless things get worse, and that things will not get worse unless they are elected. Liberals retort that the conservative approach is simply a mandate for selfishness.

I trust this clarifies the subject of the distribution of wealth. The underlying premise is that everybody ought to have a piece of the action, a slice of the pie, because we all deserve the good life.

It is my conviction that Deuteronomy has some things to say on the subject, but on a level which is rarely addressed in political rhetoric and economic debate.

Because you may not be too familiar with the Book of Deuteronomy, we may need to do some groundwork. As we look at the five verses at the beginning of chapter 1, I'm going to ask some very simple questions: "Who said it?" "What did he say?" "Whom did he say it to?" "Where did he say it?" "When did he say it?" "Why did he say it?"

I am introducing this rather prosaic portion of Scripture to show you that simple questions addressed to even a dull passage can reap tremendous benefits.

Who Said It?

Verse 1 says, "These are the words Moses spoke." If we are to rightly understand the significance of these words, then we need to know a little bit about the person, Moses.

● Moses was extraordinarily gifted. You remember that in the early days of the Christian church, the first martyr was a man called Stephen, who had been appointed deacon. Apparently he got his "deacing" done quite quickly and so he took to preaching. He became a phenomenal preacher who elicited a powerful response from the people. Nobody was neutral when Stephen preached! In the end those against him outnumbered those for him, and they decided to kill him. Before they did, however, he gave a closing speech which was a brilliant and brief overview of the history of the people of Israel. It is recorded for us in Acts 7. This is what he said about Moses, "At that time Moses was born, and he was no ordinary child. For three months he was cared for in his father's house. When he was placed outside, Pharaoh's daughter took him and brought him up as her own son. Moses was educated in all the wisdom of the Egyptians and was powerful in speech and action" (Acts 7:20-22).

You may remember that at the time Moses was born, Pha-

11

raoh dealt harshly with the Children of Israel and insisted that all their male children should be killed. Moses' parents devised a scheme where they could get around this edict. They placed the little boy in an ark of bullrushes and floated him on the Nile among the crocodiles. When Pharaoh's daughter came down to the river, she found the baby and adopted him. And so Moses, the Hebrew child, actually became part of the royal family of the Pharaoh who wanted to have him done away with. In this privileged position he was educated in all the wisdom of the Egyptians.

Now a lot of people seem to think that because people lived a few thousand years ago they were a bunch of dummies or, in the case of the Egyptians, mummies. This, of course, is far from the truth. Those of you who have traveled in Egypt, as I have, have seen some of the wonders of the pyramids. If you study the mathematics of the pyramids, you will recognize that it is no exaggeration to say that there are very few people in the United States who could even start to figure out the mathematics of the pyramids. The Egyptians' strengths in engineering were phenomenal. When you look at the sheer bulk and the size of those pyramids you wonder how in the world they built them; and when you study illustrations of their methods, you still hardly credit that they could do it. They were brilliant people and Moses was absolutely trained by the best. We see his facility with language as we read the Book of Deuteronomy. The historian Josephus tells us that when the Ethiopians and the Egyptians went to war, it was Moses who commanded the troops of Egypt and brought about a great military victory. And, of course, we know that he was the one God called to bring the people of Israel out of Egypt. For forty years he led them in a hopeless situation and eventually brought the people to the verge of the Promised Land, only to be told to then hand them over to his young aide, Joshua.

● Moses was supernaturally called. When he was forty years

old, he got into trouble with the authorities and had to flee for his life. He went out into the desert and took to raising sheep. Having lived at the height of the intellectual and political world, and in the lap of luxury, he now spent forty years in a pastoral situation raising his family. And then God came to him. After forty years had passed, an angel appeared to Moses in the flames of the burning bush in the desert near Mount Sinai. When he saw this he was amazed at the sight; and as he went over to look more closely he heard the Lord's voice saying, "I am the God of your father, the God of Abraham, the God of Isaac and the God of Jacob." Moses trembled with fear and did not dare to look at the bush. The Lord also said to him, "I have indeed seen the misery of My people in Egypt. I have heard them crying out because of their slave-drivers, and I am concerned about their suffering" (Exodus 3:6-7). God then began to unveil His eternal purposes as they related to Moses. He planned to rescue His people in Egypt but He needed a man who would be the leader; and so He went to the back of the desert and called this brilliant and wonderfully gifted man and said, "I'm going to send you back to Egypt."

But Moses was less than enthusiastic. He began to deliver a catalog of excuses about why he should not go. Whenever you need an excuse not to get involved in the Lord's work, remember, you will never think of an original one. Moses thought of them all first. In the end God became irritated with him and told him in no uncertain words to go down to Egypt and get on with the job. So powerful was the call of God in his life that he went, despite his trepidation and reluctance.

• Moses was uniquely privileged. He was a man with whom God spoke face-to-face (Exodus 33:11). When Miriam and Aaron, his sister and brother, began to criticize him behind his back—which is the usual place that critics operate—God overheard their criticism and had a word for them. He told them in effect, "Get off his back; that man Moses is My man." God added that when He wanted to communicate with people, He usually spoke through a prophet; but with Moses He spoke face-to-face. Moses had an intimate and unique relationship with the living God.

● Moses was unusually devoted. Hebrews 11 records a list of people who were the heroes of the faith. Moses fits well in such company. It is said of him,

By faith Moses, when he had grown up, refused to be known as the son of Pharaoh's daughter. He chose to be mistreated along with the people of God rather than to enjoy the pleasures of sin for a short time. He regarded disgrace for the sake of Christ of greater value than the treasures of Egypt, because he was looking ahead to his reward. By faith he left Egypt, not fearing the king's anger; he persevered because he saw Him who is invisible (Hebrews 11:24-27).

What a remarkable statement concerning Moses' devotion. He had the opportunity to be known as the son of Pharaoh's daughter, and yet turned away from that heritage. He had the opportunity to enjoy the favor and the blessings of Pharaoh's court, but chose rather to identify with the downtrodden people of God. He chose the wrath of Pharaoh because he saw past it to Him who is invisible. Moses had a sense of the eternal; he understood that God was greater than Pharaoh and that the purposes of God were infinitely more significant than all the wealth of this world.

If you came across such a man, I'm sure you'd love to spend time with him. That being impossible, the next best thing would be to have something that he wrote. You'd read it, wouldn't you? Well, you've got it — it's called Deuteronomy.

What Did He Say?
Two answers are readily available. "Moses proclaimed to the Israelites all that the Lord had commanded him concerning

14

them," and, "Moses began to expound this law" (vv. 3, 5). It's a wonderful thing to believe in a God who is high, holy and transcendent, far above and remote, removed from all sin and degradation and the pettiness of mankind. It's even more wonderful to believe that such a God is not so remote that He is unknowable or so far removed that He is unreachable. It is truly amazing that God is willing to communicate from His holiness to mankind in language that can be understood, and with something of practical significance that requires our response. That is the whole point of Moses telling the people all that the Lord had commanded him to say. God was intimately concerned about them, speaking to them, giving them practical instructions and outlining His glorious promises.

Notice the word "expound" in verse 5. The Hebrew word is translated quite differently in Deuteronomy 27:8, where instructions are given concerning the carving of the words of God on the tablets of stone; it says they must be carved "very clearly." That's the real meaning of expound—to take the truth and so articulate it that it becomes abundantly clear. Then the people will have no excuses; they cannot escape or avoid what is being said. This is the task of the expositor, the expounder of the Word of God.

Along with the Children of Israel, we can listen to this extraordinarily gifted, supernaturally called and uniquely privileged, and unusually devoted man, Moses, and recognize that he is really bringing to us in crystal clear terms what God has to say to His people. We'll listen, won't we? Particularly when we realize that the subject is "the good life."

Whom Did He Say It To?

"These are the words Moses spoke to all Israel" (v. 1). The expression "all Israel" occurs over and over again in the book of Deuteronomy. You see God was speaking not just to people who were doing their individual thing; He was speaking to a group that recognized they were the people of God. This is a salutary reminder to those of us who seek for the good life today. Our intention usually is to find the good life "for me!" But what kind of good life is found in the community of which you are a part?

When Ronald Reagan was running against Jimmy Carter in 1980, he asked the American people, "Are you better off now than you were four years ago?" That really goes to the heart of the matter, because basically, that's what most people want. Am I, personally, individually, better off than I was four years ago? When God speaks to all Israel He is not asking them, "Are you, personally, better off than you were four years ago?" What He is asking is, "Are you enjoying the good life more in the community in which I have placed you? And are you concerned to see this community living under the blessing of God?"

Israel was a *covenant* community. This meant that God had made very special commitments to them and He expected them to respond. They were also a *chosen* community. God had not chosen them because there was something special about them, or because they were very strong, or even numerous. He had sovereignly chosen them to be the conduit of His blessing to all the nations of the world. When we think of the good life as God defines good, we recognize that the question is not whether I am better off than I was four years ago. Rather, the challenge is that I might so live before God that the people to whom I belong, and the people for whom I have a responsibility, might be blessed because I am living in the fullness of the blessing of the Gospel.

Where Did He Say It?

"These are the words Moses spoke to all Israel in the desert east of the Jordan" (v. 1). East of the Jordan indicates that they had come right up to the borders of the Promised Land and then stayed there for a long time. Let me remind you of the circumstances. When God sent Moses into Egypt to bring the people out of captivity, His intention was that they should move quickly through the desert and into the Promised Land. Unfortunately, when they came to the borders of the Promised Land under Moses' direction, there were people who chose not to trust or obey God.

As a result of their rebellion, they wandered in the wilderness for forty years; but in that period something very interesting had happened. God had decreed that the people who had refused to go into the Promised Land would never, ever enter it. Instead they would spend forty years wandering aimlessly around an area that it would take eleven days to traverse. Forty years doing an eleven-day journey! What was happening in the forty years? During this time a whole generation of the rebellious was dying and a new generation was being born. So when Moses stood poised on the verge of the Promised Land with his hundreds of thousands of people ready to go in and enjoy the good life that God had for them, he was standing before the people who had been born within the last forty years. They were the baby boomers!

When Did He Say It?

He said this forty years after they had turned back from entering the Promised Land, during which time they had gone round in circles in the wilderness. How on earth can you take forty years to do an eleven-day journey? It reminds me of the story of the Texan talking to an old Scottish farmer. The Texan said to the farmer, "How many acres do you have on your ranch?" He said, "About fifteen." "Fifteen acres—you call that a ranch?" "No, sir, I didn't call it a ranch; you called it a ranch." "Back home in Texas on my ranch I get up in the morning, get in my automobile, I drive all day and at the end of the day I'm still on my ranch." The Scotsman said, "Yes, I had an automobile like that and I got rid of it." I doubt if an old Scotsman in his old automobile could take forty years on an eleven-day journey in the wilderness! These people had grumbled, they had growled, they had griped, they had rebelled, they had resisted, but during the forty years they had discovered two things.

• The unshakable faithfulness of God

• The inevitability of the consequences of your actions catching up with you.

It is to people who have learned those lessons, and who are now poised for something much better, that Moses speaks.

You too may be hurting; you may have gone through difficult times. You may have grumbled, perhaps you rebelled and resisted; no doubt, you are living with some of the consequences of your actions. The good news, of course, is that God offers the good life to people just like you.

Why Did He Say it?

The answer to that question is threefold. As we read Deuteronomy we're going to hear Moses carefully recounting the *history* of the people of Israel. People of God always need a sense of history—a reminder of what God has done. You see, God is not an ethereal being, remote and removed from us, unconcerned about us. He has consistently acted in the history of His chosen people and, in "these last days He has spoken to us by His Son" (Hebrews 1:2). He invaded time and space and became rooted in our history. What He did in Christ's incarnation is historically verifiable. He is not asking us to believe a lot of things that cannot be authenticated; He is saying, "I have laid aside My deity and have assumed your humanity, and I have moved into your society and the evidence is there. I have shown you what I am like, and you can see and understand what I've done. Look at what I have done down through the centuries." God's people always need a sense of history.

But notice that Moses is also talking about the future, to give them a sense of *destiny*. For if we have a solid footing on the understanding of what God has done in history, we find hope and encouragement in our destiny which God has planned. We need to be alert to all that God has promised His people out of His grace and goodness.

God also wanted to give them a sense of *responsibility*. For if we have that solid base of history, and if we have that keen anticipation of destiny, the big question is, "What is our responsibility in between the two?" Our responsibility is to respond to God according to that which He has clearly, unmistakably enunciated to us. As we do that, we begin to discover how to enjoy the good life.

B ut you were unwilling to go up; you rebelled against the command of the Lord your God. You grumbled in your tents and said, 'The Lord hates us; so He brought us out of Egypt to deliver us into the hands of the Amorites to destroy us. Where can we go? Our brothers have made us lose heart. They say, "The people are stronger and taller than we are; the cities are large, with walls up to the sky. We even saw the Anakites there." '

"Then I said to you, 'Do not be terrified; do not be afraid of them. The Lord your God, who is going before you, will fight for you, as He did for you in Egypt, before your very eyes, and in the desert. There you saw how the Lord your God carried you, as a father carries his son, all the way you went until you reached this place.'

"In spite of this, you did not trust in the Lord your God, who went ahead of you on your journey, in fire by night and in a cloud by day, to search out places for you to camp and to show you the way you should go."

Deuteronomy 1:26-33

THE LORD OUR GOD – THE KEY TO THE GOOD LIFE

2 "The Lord our God" is a constantly recurring expression in Deuteronomy. If you want a succinct statement of what Deuteronomy is all about, it would be "How to relate to the Lord our God." This is the key to understanding the book and also the secret to enjoying the good life. If we are to live the good life and enjoy it to the full, the key is to rightly relate to the Lord our God.

Recognizing the Lord Our God

Everybody has a god of some kind. Man is incorrigibly religious. There is, as Augustine said, a God-shaped vacuum inside everybody, and they try to fill that space with all manner of things or people or ideas or interests. All of us have an inner sense that we are inadequate, that we need more. And the "more" that we look for becomes our god. Many people focus their need on a religious object and discover God in a spiritual sense. But many more are purely secular in their search. Even assuming that we are religiously inclined, we need to remind ourselves that it is possible for us to have a god who is the product of our own imagination, who exists nowhere except in the realm of our own fantasies.

Let me give you an example of this. One day when Jesus was walking toward Caesarea-Philippi with His disciples, He turned to them and asked them the results of the latest opinion poll concerning Him. They gave various answers. Then He asked the $64,000 question, "But who do you say that I am?" And Peter answered, "You are the Christ." At last, Peter got an answer right! Then to his dismay the Lord said to him, "Don't dare tell anybody." Now that was very, very hard for Peter. Why was he forbidden to say anything? The reason became clear as Jesus explained more about Himself. He said the Son of Man would be rejected, must suffer and die, and on the third day would rise again. And Peter's response to all this was an emphatic "NO!" He did not want a Christ who would suffer, be rejected, die, or rise again from the dead.

Who then was the Christ that Peter honored? A Christ who did not exist. He fit comfortably into Peter's preconceptions, but in terms of reality, there was no such Christ. When we talk about the Lord our God, we must be sure He isn't a God we have made up, but the One who exists eternally and who has taken the initiative to reveal Himself to mankind.

Recognizing God's Character

When you see the word LORD, you are seeing a translation of the Hebrew word *Jahve* or *Jehovah*. When you see Lord, you are reading the English equivalent for the Hebrew word *Adonai*. When Moses speaks repeatedly about "the LORD our God," he is talking about Jehovah.

When Moses was commissioned by God to bring the Children of Israel out of Egypt, he wriggled a whole lot until he discovered that he really couldn't get out of it. Since he had to go, he asked the great question, "Who should I say sent me?"

And the Lord answered him, "Say I AM has sent you."

Can you imagine Moses' response? If he had been British he would have said, "I beg Your pardon?" If he had been

American, he would have said, "Huh? I AM has sent me? What do You mean I AM has sent me? I asked, What is Your name?"

"I AM that I AM."

Moses caught on eventually. He had asked God for His name and God had told him. I AM that I AM was His name! Now I AM and *Jehovah* are related. *Jehovah* is such a holy name that Jewish people won't even articulate it. It is related to the verb "to be" and means that God IS. Not so much that He was, or that He will be, but that HE IS. This gives us the sense that He is eternal, transcending all things. "I AM that I AM" means, "Nothing is going to change Me. I am self-existent. I am self-contained. I am sufficient. I am utterly, distinctly other. I am beyond comprehension. I have no beginning, I have no end, I just am."

All these strange, mysterious, eternal, grand concepts are wrapped up in the name LORD/*Jehovah*. One of the great needs in religious circles today is for us to get back to an understanding of what God-centered religion is all about. The kind of religion we're into right now is often more man-centered than God-centered. Man with all his needs is the focus, and God floats around the periphery dancing attendance on those needs, meeting our whims and ministering to our caprices. We have become the focal point instead of the Lord, the Eternal One, the One who transcends all things, totally other, complete and entire in Himself. The Lord was the key to the Children of Israel entering the Promised Land.

The word God translates the Hebrew word ELOHIM which is the plural of EL. As EL means God and ELOHIM is plural, some people see in this word a hint of the Trinity, and that may be part of what is intended here. More likely, however, the idea of the plural word is to show intensity and grandness.

The British perhaps understand this better, because we have had a royal family for years. When the Queen speaks authoritatively, she never says "I," but always "We." It is known as the "Royal We." There is a sense of majesty and dignity about it. Here is somebody who is larger than life, who is grander than the rest, who is to be deeply respected and honored. So when we think in terms of GOD, LORD, JEHOVAH, ELOHIM, we're thinking of the self-existent, eternal, utterly transcendent Lord, who in the intensity and the uniqueness of His awesome being desires and deserves and demands our reverent allegiance.

It should be noted that when Moses prayed he used another title, "O Sovereign LORD" (Deuteronomy 3:24). This translates the word *Adonai,* once again intensifying the thought of God but adding the idea of His majesty. The words *Jehovah, Elohim,* and *Adonai* combine to picture God totally complete in Himself, sovereignly in control, utterly other, majestically dealing with the affairs of the world, desiring, demanding, deserving our allegiance.

Some years ago J.B. Phillips wrote a book called *Your God Is Too Small.* For years I never had time to read it, but I thoroughly enjoyed the title! But eventually I read the book which pinpoints the all-too-common problem in our lives — that our God is too small. We have lost the sense of *Jehovah, Elohim, Adonai.*

Recognizing God's Covenant

The apparently insignificant word "our" is sandwiched between "Lord" and "God." If the statements concerning God's character tend to make Him seem remote and removed from us, the little word "our" changes all that. Here we have the other side of who God is. He is transcendent, but He is also immanent. He is noble, but He is reachable, a God who can be experienced. He isn't just "the Lord God." He certainly isn't just "the man upstairs." He isn't just "our Maker." He is the Lord God who can be ours, personally and intimately.

Why is this? He can be known as our God because He is the

One who has made some very definite commitments to the fathers — to Abraham, Isaac, Jacob, and their descendants. In addition to talking about "the Lord our God," Moses also speaks about "the Lord, the God of our fathers," reminding the people of their long history in which God had moved in their affairs and made Himself uniquely and personally "their" God. He had done this by way of covenants. The word "covenant" is sometimes translated "testament." The two divisions of the Bible which we call Old Testament and New Testament could equally be called Old Covenant and New Covenant. Therefore, it is rather obvious that one of the dominant themes of Scripture is that God is a God of covenants. Now what does this mean?

In recent years scholars have researched the kinds of treaties made in Old Testament times and have discovered something fascinating. In those days, every little city had its own king, and his power and prestige was directly related to the size of the city. So you might have a small city with a king, and five miles down the road another small city with a king, and the two kings might not get along together. If one of them decided to clobber the other, then he would become bigger, because he would be king of two cities. And if he got the idea, "Hey, I like this," and went around clobbering the other kings, he would in the end become big, and all the little kings would be frightened of him. Then if he started to flex his muscles, the little kings would come to him and say, "Listen, don't clobber us. Please be our *suzerain* and we will be your *vassals.* For our purposes, *suzerain* is "big king" and *vassal* is "little king." A suzerainty treaty was an agreement, whereby the "big king" would say to a "little king," "I will protect you, I will care for you, I will provide for you, I will rule over you, I will reign in your affairs. You can enjoy all that I will make available to you, and all I ask of you is your loyalty and allegiance. You will demonstrate that by trusting me and obeying me."

As scholars researched the covenants we read of in Scripture, they discovered marked similarities to the suzerainty treaties. So let's apply this now. The Big King, God, has come to the little king, Israel, and has said, "I will care for you, I will protect you, I will provide for you, I will carry you, I will uphold you, I will fight for you. I will be your God, and the only thing I ask of you is your loyalty and allegiance, which will be demonstrated in your trust of Me and your obedience to Me." That is the idea of covenant that runs from one end of the Bible to the other.

In Genesis 9 there was a terrible Flood, and at the end of the Flood God had a word with Noah to say, "I make My covenant with you. (Big King talking to little king.) And this is My covenant—I will never again destroy mankind by a flood. And so that you will know I have made this promise, I will set My bow in the sky, so that every time you see a rainbow you will remember My covenant." That is not to suggest that the rainbow did not exist before then, but that God now imparted specific significance to it. Notice that God took the initiative in making a promise; now people could lay hold of the promise or could live terrified and refuse to accept the covenant.

God Making a Covenant with Abraham

Abraham was living in Ur of the Chaldees, a remarkably civilized city. One day God tapped him on the shoulder and said, "Abraham, I want you to go to a land that I will show you after you get there." It is amazing that Abraham left Ur of the Chaldees on such limited information. When he finally arrived at the land God wanted to show him, he found hostile territory populated by pagan tribes—a most unpromising situation compared to the one he had left behind. One day God said to him, "Look at the stars of the sky and at the sand of the sea. I will make your descendants just as numerous." When Abraham pointed out that he was very old and didn't have the first descendant yet, God told him, "Don't worry about that. I will make a covenant with you. Look where the soles of your feet are and look where you've walked — I will give you this land." Abraham responded, "I've only got a handful of men. How in the world are You going to do that with all these pagan tribes around me?" God replied, "I am your shield and your very great reward" (Genesis 15:1).

Big King talked to little king and little king believed God. He accepted all these remarkable things that Big King promised him. He believed it and it was reckoned to him for righteousness.

God Making a Covenant with Israel

More than 430 years later, the Children of Israel having been brought out of Egypt with a mighty deliverance, have taken a brief hiatus in their journey at Mount Sinai (or Horeb). There God met with Moses and filled out the details of the covenant, "You will be My special people, you will be My treasured possession, you will be a kingdom of priests, you will have the land I promised to your father Abraham, and to Isaac and to Jacob. When you get into the land, you are going to behave as My people; I give you My covenant, and I'll give you My commandments." When the people heard about the covenant and the commandments they responded, "We will obey the covenant and the commandments."

The Big King who had given the covenant to Noah and had amplified it for Abraham, sharply focused it now for Moses who passed it on to the people. With this covenant in mind, they embarked on their journey to the Promised Land.

Now what was the point of all this? Simply that if they were going to enjoy the good life, they would need to rightly relate to the Lord their God. But if they were going to rightly relate to the Lord their God, they must also understand His character and gladly respond to His covenants. The tragic history of the people of Israel shows that although they were

constantly reminded of the Lord their God and His covenant,
they ignored Him and broke covenant. The prophets would
come to remind them, and they would repent and there would
be revival, and then they would drift back to their old ways. In
the end the Prophet Jeremiah told the people,

> "The time is coming," declares the Lord, "when I will
> make a new covenant with the house of Israel and with
> the house of Judah.
> "It will not be like the covenant I made with their
> forefathers when I took them by the hand to lead them
> out of Egypt, because they broke My covenant, though I
> was a husband to them," declares the Lord.
> "This is the covenant I will make with the house of
> Israel after that time," declares the Lord. "I will put My
> law in their minds and write it on their hearts. I will be
> their God, and they will be My people. No longer will a
> man teach his neighbor, or a man his brother, saying,
> 'Know the Lord'; because they will all know Me, from
> the least of them to the greatest," declares the Lord.
> "For I will forgive their wickedness and will remember
> their sins no more" (Jeremiah 31:31-34).

Through Jeremiah God was saying that there would be a
new covenant coming; it was not that the old one was bad,
but that people were not prepared or able to respond adequately to it. The new covenant would not only outline for
people who God is and what He would give them and provide
for them, but God would also put His laws in their hearts and
write His precepts in their minds. In other words, God's laws
wouldn't be externally imposed upon a reluctant people but
would be internally impressed, so that they would begin to
delight in them, and long to fulfill them. Not only that, the
people wouldn't be searching after God; they would know
Him. They would recognize that He had forgiven their sins.

This new covenant found its fulfillment in our Lord Jesus Christ, for through His work on the cross, and by the ministry of the Holy Spirit, we can have a new mind, a new heart, and forgiveness of sins. We can know the Lord and can rejoice in being His people and enjoy the good life He has promised in His covenant to us.

Responding to the Lord Our God

It is one thing to recognize the Lord our God, but it is an entirely different thing to respond to Him properly. Moses instructed the people, "See the Lord your God has given you the land. Go up and take possession of it as the Lord, the God of your fathers, told you. Do not be afraid; do not be discouraged" (Deuteronomy 1:21). It's one thing to have the land laid out before you, but it's an entirely different thing to go in and live in the good of it. It's one thing to have the covenant God offers you in Christ — all spiritual blessings in heavenly places; it's an entirely different thing to go in and take possession of the blessings. Therein lies the key to the good life — to recognize who the Lord your God is, to accept the covenant He has made with you, and then, recognizing what He has given, to press in to take possession of it.

This response requires an attitude which says, "Covenant God, Sovereign Lord, Suzerain Majesty, here I am. I need Your protection, I need Your care, I need Your direction. I need a new heart, I need a new mind, I need new aspirations. I need to be made a new creation. I need forgiveness of sins."

The Sovereign Lord replies, "I have made My covenant to you in Christ; it's yours, take it, move in and possess it, and live in the good of it."

The remarkable thing is that forty years earlier the people had arrived at this very point on the edge of the Promised Land and had seen it stretching out before them, but had failed to go in and enjoy it. Why? Because somebody came back and said, "Hey, there are some big giants there," and the people responded, "If there are some big giants there, let's not try at all." They were afraid and easily discouraged.

The good life is not without battles, not without struggles. The good life does not mean that everything will be handed to you on a silver platter. The good life means that in the covenant, God offers you Himself and all that you need in Christ, and then simply tells you that you will enjoy all that He is and all that He has in the normal context where the world, the flesh, and the devil militate against the purposes of God. He says that He will give you the good life, but it will be in the context of the fallenness of man and the fallenness of the society you have created and the fallenness of the world that you inhabit. It's going to be a struggle.

Many people battle with the world and they battle with the flesh and they battle with the devil, and in the end they give up and say, "The giants are too big for us." They are afraid to do it God's way. Often their hands are so full, holding on to things of little significance that they don't have room to possess all that God offers them.

One day I took my little grandson, Danny, a coloring book. I was eager to give it to the little guy, but when I got there I saw that he was holding a toy train in one hand and a blanket in the other and had a football under one arm and a Green Bay Packer helmet under the other. The poor little guy had his hands so full of stuff that he couldn't receive my present. He was unable to enjoy what I was offering him.

Therein lies the problem of people who never relate properly to the Lord their God. They don't understand what He has given in His covenant. They don't realize it must be possessed, and they are afraid to let go of what they are clutching, fearing that if they do, God will short-change them.

Resisting the Lord Our God

Of course the Children of Israel *intended* to follow God, but over time, they actually went to the extreme of resisting Him.

Moses' strategy in recounting their sad history was so that the next generation could learn from the mistakes of an earlier one. This is what he says about them, "They rebelled against the Lord. . . . They resented the challenges of the Lord. . . . They refused to trust the Lord. . . . They resisted the servants of the Lord. . . . They received the consequences of their own lack of faith and disobedience" (vv. 26-37).

Every generation needs to be warned by the shortcomings of the previous generation. All of us need to learn from the history of those who have pressed on to enjoy all that the Covenant God makes available to us. We also need to read, mark, learn, and inwardly digest the lessons of what happens in the lives of the disobedient and the unfaithful.

The Lord your God, Jehovah, self-existent, without beginning and end, entire, complete in Himself, needing nothing, majestic, sovereign, ruling in the affairs of this world has deigned to humble Himself to reach out in covenant promise to us in His Son. And He invites you to move in response to His covenant, in faith and obedience, demonstrating your loyalty and your obedience to Him. He promises to fight for you, He promises to carry you, He promises to lead you. You have two options: you can resist the Lord your God or you can respond to Him. And the difference will be simply this—you'll either enjoy the good life or you won't. The key is the Lord your God.

At that time I said to you, 'You are too heavy a burden for me to carry alone. The Lord your God has increased your numbers so that today you are as many as the stars in the sky. May the Lord, the God of your fathers, increase you a thousand times and bless you as He has promised! But how can I bear your problems and your burdens and your disputes all by myself? Choose some wise, understanding and respected men from each of your tribes, and I will set them over you.'

"You answered me, 'What you propose is good.'

"So I took the leading men of your tribes, wise and respected men, and appointed them to have authority over you — as commanders of thousands, of hundreds, of fifties and of tens and as tribal officials. And I charged your judges at that time: 'Hear the disputes between your brothers and judge fairly, whether the case is between brother Israelites or between one of them and an alien. Do not show partiality in judging; hear both small and great alike. Do not be afraid of any man, for judgment belongs to God. Bring me any case too hard for you, and I will hear it.' And at that time I told you everything you were to do."

Deuteronomy 1:9-18

SHARING THE GOOD LIFE

3 Here is a trivia question. What was the name of Moses' father-in-law? He was a very important man, even if he isn't very well known. His name was Jethro and the reason he is important is because he gave some absolutely wonderful advice to Moses. Without this advice Moses might not have survived. Not only that, when Jethro's advice was put into operation, it made all the difference in the world for the Children of Israel, and is still applicable to the cause of Christ and to the people of God.

This was the situation. One day Jethro went to visit Moses in the wilderness. Some Bible students estimate that Moses was looking after no less than 2 million people, although the figure isn't specifically mentioned in Scripture. We do know that there were 600,000 men over twenty years of age who were capable of going to war. While he was visiting the family, Jethro wondered where Moses was all day and so he went to see. He discovered that Moses left at the crack of dawn and got back in the dead of night, and was spending all his waking hours dealing with the problems and the burdens and the disputes of 2 million people! One day Jethro said to his son-in-law, "If you go on like this, my daughter is going to be a widow and I don't particularly want to take her under my wing again. We are going to have to do something about you. Also, despite all your hard work, these people are not being cared for properly. I perceive there are two problems: How to care for the people and how to bear the load. So let's sit down and figure out how the people can be properly cared for and how the burden you are carrying can be properly shared."

The same two problems exist in the church today. Jethro's answer to Moses is echoed in the New Testament, where we learn that those who are in leadership in the church are required to be equipping the congregation to do the work of the ministry. And the people in the congregation are to see themselves as privileged people who share the load. Somewhere along the line, somebody got the idea that "church" means a large group of lay people paying a small group of professionals to do the ministry. This idea is unbiblical and impractical. The way the church is supposed to work is that those in positions of leadership are to encourage and motivate, and to mobilize the people in the pews to be involved in the caring and sharing.

The Immensity of the Problem—Caring for Everyone
● The numerical problems. Moses had led the people out of Egypt, across the Red Sea, into the wilderness and up to the borders of the Promised Land. Moses was not grumbling that there were 2 million of them; in fact, he saw this as an evidence of divine blessing. You'll notice he said, "The Lord your God has increased your numbers so that today you are as many as the stars in the sky" (1:10). The expression he used is almost identical to one God used as a promise to Abraham. When God made His covenant with Abraham, He promised among other things that He would make his descendants as numerous as the stars in the sky. From Moses' point of view, the reason there were so many of them was because God had kept His covenant promise and had worked in their lives.

To give you an idea of how wonderfully God had worked, remember that before God could bring the people of Israel out of Egypt, He had to get them there first. How did He do that? He sent one man—Joseph. Then he sent Joseph's extended family—seventy people. In 430 years, the seventy had become 2 million! If you prefer mathematics to theology, get your pocket calculator out and figure out how many children they would have needed per family to grow from seventy to 2 million in 430 years! Each family needed to produce an average of three sons and three daughters. I didn't work it out— Frans Delitzsch, the German theologian did! That's the sort of thing German theologians do.

The point is that God had protected them and provided for them. He had preserved them and had brought them through innumerable difficulties, and now they were a vast evidence of divine blessing. But they needed handling. I suggest to you that whenever God blesses numerically, whenever He brings people into the kingdom, that is always something to rejoice about and something to worry about. For the more people He brings into the kingdom, the more blessing He pours out on the society in which we live, the more problems have to be addressed. And there were immense numerical problems here.

• The social problems. Because a whole generation died in the wilderness, we know that somebody had to conduct thousands of funerals. Who did it? After the funerals, the bereaved had to be comforted. Who did that? When people got sick, who did the hospital visitation—such as it was? Who coped with people who got snakebites, those who didn't handle their diets as instructed by Moses, and those who didn't follow the sanitary laws God had outlined? Sickness, illness, death, bereavement—immense problems that somebody had to cope with. But there were other unique social problems.

Did you know that when the people of Israel were slaves in Egypt they were allowed to own slaves themselves? Can you imagine what it must have been like to be a slave of a slave?

Talk about being on the bottom of the totem pole! There were a lot of these people in the wilderness. Yet, how could a Hebrew possibly have become the slave of a slave? In those days if you were in business and someone owed you money but was unable to pay even after they had sold everything, there was another provision for the payment of debt. According to Hebrew law, as a last resort the debtor could sell his children and wives and himself into slavery to pay off his debts. A Hebrew slave of a Hebrew had confronted total financial disaster, and was utterly and completely destitute.

There were also specific provisions for widows. Not only had they lost their husbands, but because of the particular attitude to women and the specific inheritance laws that were in place at the time, widows were in danger of total abandonment. Their sense of utter helplessness, compounded by excruciating loneliness and their need of protection, meant that somebody had to look out for them. There must have been thousands of them with all those people who died in the wilderness, bearing in mind that men seem to die younger than women.

Then there was another group of people in this vast crowd. In the *King James Bible* they are called a "mixed multitude." In the *New International Version* they are called by the uncomplimentary term "rabble." They didn't really belong to the people of God, but had decided to leave Egypt and to go along anyway. Probably they had been watching the great contest between Moses, as representative of Jehovah, and the magicians of Pharaoh, and had seen Jehovah's man win hands down. They weren't really interested in God and they really weren't interested in the people of God, and they weren't interested in the Promised Land; they just went along because they were peripherally interested; but there they were in the wilderness with Moses. The "rabble" and "widows" and "slaves" are all mentioned in Deuteronomy, and they all had to be cared for.

● The personal problems. Moses said to the people, "You are too heavy a burden for me to carry alone. . . . How can I bear your problems and your burdens and your disputes all by myself?" (1:9, 12) The people, corporately, had become an immense burden. Individually, they were carrying all kinds of burdens. When you have burdened individuals, they become a burden corporately, and you've got burdens upon burdens upon burdens. Moses was trying to bear these burdens alone. In the end he said, "I've had it. There is absolutely no way that I can cope with all the burdens and problems and disputes that are represented in this vast crowd of people."

This word "burden" is worth a closer look. The psalmist says, "My guilt has overwhelmed me like a burden too heavy to bear" (Psalm 38:4). There are people in every society who are burdened with guilt. This burden is playing itself out in all kinds of ways in their behavior. It is affecting them physiologically, psychologically, and relationally, and unless somebody gets to them and helps them to alleviate the burden of guilt, they may experience dire problems themselves and cause utter chaos in their relationships. Now I'm not talking about the false guilt caused by self-imposed unrealistic expectations or by dysfunctional families. I'm talking about the genuine guilt we feel when the Spirit of God says we have sinned and when, like the psalmist, we repress it instead of confessing and turning from our sin, and knowing forgiveness. We press it down inside us and there it begins to work like a spiritual cancer. The psalmist said that he felt he was totally parched and totally empty and utterly dissatisfied and unfulfilled. That is exactly the position of many people today. They are carrying a burden of guilt that has not been addressed. Somebody needs to minister to them.

The word "burden" is also used in 2 Samuel 15:33 as an illustration of the sheer weight of circumstances. The story is of King David who discovers to his dismay that his beloved son Absalom is a traitor, out to capture his father's kingdom and, if necessary, to take his father's life. Imagine circumstances like that! David has to flee from the palace and he goes down over the Kidron Valley and climbs up the side of the Mount of Olives to head down into the wilderness by the Dead Sea. And as he arrives at the top of the Mount of Olives, he meets his friend, Hushai, who volunteers to travel into exile with him. But David says to him, "I just can't cope with taking you along with me; you would just be a burden to me." Can you imagine circumstances so bad that even friends become a burden?

Then there is the "burden" of Job as described in Job 7:20. Admittedly, the Hebrew can be interpreted different ways, but one translation reads, "I have become a burden to myself." People who start talking like that are in danger of slipping into dangerous depression. Somebody has got to look after them. Moses was trying to bear all these burdens from morning to night, and his father-in-law looked at him and said, "Before very long my daughter is going to be a widow and these folks aren't going to be looked after anyway. We've got to do something about this."

• The spiritual problems. Some of the people coming to Moses were anxiously seeking God's will (Exodus 18:15). Now this is an entirely different situation. Some people bring the most unbelievable problems, and some people come because they get into the most unbelievable fights, and some people who come have become involved in unbelievably complex tangles. But there are some who come with a totally different concern and say, "God has been speaking to me. I have a sense that He is leading me, but I need some godly advice. Will you please help me find God's will?"

It is so exciting to meet people who say, "I don't have a problem, I don't have a difficulty, I just need some advice." But talking with them still takes time. Nobody can be anybody else's Holy Spirit. We can outline biblical principles and give certain scriptural directives; but in the long run, they have to be brought to the point of feeling, before God, that they understand His will. We can minister, we can share, we can encourage, we can teach — and what a delight it is to be able to minister in this way to those who are responsive and who need direction. But it takes time.

Of course, there were also those who fought God's will. For everyone who sought it, there were probably half a dozen who fought it! Those who were responsive needed direction, but those who were rebellious needed correction. There are few things so tiring as having to deal with people who are fighting God's will. Moses was trying to stand tall and tell them, "Thus saith the Lord." But some of the people were resistant to it and Moses was trying to warn them, "Listen, unless you turn from the error of your ways, there are going to be all kinds of unfortunate consequences."

Then there were, as there are today, those who doubt God's will, the ambivalent people. They weren't responsive and they weren't rebellious; they were flip-flopping in between. One day they would get up and say, "Not my will, but Thine be done, O Lord." And the next day they would say, "Not Thy will, but mine be done, O Lord." These people need protection, because if they are not very careful, they are going to get themselves into problems.

Who gives the correction, the direction, and the protection? Well, Moses was trying to do it all himself.

● The attitudinal problems. It would have been bad enough trying to cope with all these people and the immensity of their problems if everybody had been sweet and cooperative. Unfortunately, all was not sweetness and light. There were all kinds of attitudinal problems as well. Some people were getting bent out of shape. The "rabble" were a thorn in Moses' flesh from day one because they were forever grumbling. It wasn't just that they grumbled among themselves. As is usually the case, a grumbler needs an audience. The audience enjoys listening to the grumbling and becomes a grumbling audience and the grumbles rumble. Instead of appreciating Moses and his work, they started grumbling about him and what he was doing and what he wasn't doing. Obviously there were problems, all kinds of immense difficulties, but their grumbling was not helping one bit. They were simply exacerbating the problems.

There was quarreling, backbiting, and criticizing going on too, and Moses received more than his share of it. Even his brother and sister got on his case. They were upset because they thought he was getting more press than they were. They wanted to have equal time and equal billing. Now when people are jealous, they never stand up and say, "Ladies and gentlemen, I want to tell you something—I'm jealous." They find something else to say.

Miriam and Aaron began to criticize Moses' home life. Moses had married a lady they didn't approve of. That's not unusual—brothers and sisters don't always approve of their in-laws and particularly in this case, because Moses "had married a Cushite" (Numbers 12:1). Cush is the region we now call Sudan and Ethiopia, and so it is quite possible that Miriam's objections had racial overtones. Miriam made such a fuss that in the end God intervened; He made her a leper "like snow." It is tempting to wonder if God's answer to Miriam's objection to a "black" was to make the objector "whiter than white!" How do you think Moses felt? He prayed to God for his sister, but he was still called upon to deal with the bad attitudes she had stirred up.

Then along came Korah, a Levite. The Levites were a special group of people. They had been given clearly defined responsibilities, privileges and opportunities, but that wasn't enough for Korah. He wanted Aaron's job as priest and he didn't approve of Moses being in control. So he stirred up the people until they brought charges against Moses, "You've gone too far, you just want to lord it over us; you're making slaves out of us; you promised us milk and honey and you haven't delivered." (See Numbers 16:14.) Moses certainly had his hands full. No wonder he said, "You are too heavy a burden for me to carry alone."

The Simplicity of the Proposal—Sharing the Caring

Jethro told Moses, "It stands to reason that if you continue trying to handle this whole thing yourself, you'll come apart at the seams. It is equally obvious that the job isn't getting done. Therefore, the people are going to get more and more dissatisfied, and you will become more and more discouraged. I've got an idea. If you can't cope alone, you've got to share the responsibility. If you can't do all the caring, you've got to find people who will help you."

His solution was very simple—it is called *sharing the caring*. You get a lot of people to pick up what one person has been doing and the result will be as Jethro said, "You will be able to stand the strain, and all these people will go home satisfied" (Exodus 18:23). Frankly, I think Jethro was a bit of an optimist in claiming that it was possible for all the people to go home satisfied! But his proposal was sound.

● Developing a structure. Jethro insisted that the massive number of people Moses was trying to handle had to be divided into manageable groups. Then Moses would have to find people who would accept responsibility for caring for those groups and thus share the responsibility. Jethro told Moses to divide them into groups of thousands and find people who could handle a thousand people. Then he would divide the thousands into hundreds and find people who could handle a hundred; then divide the hundred into fifty and find people who could handle fifty; divide the fifties into ten and find people who could handle the ten. These leaders would deal with issues and concerns, caring personally, intimately for the people, and everybody would be responsible and accountable. Makes sense, doesn't it?

Moses was encouraged to develop leadership, but we all

know that leadership is predicated upon followership. The obvious rule of thumb is, "If they ain't following, you ain't leading." It's all right putting leaders into position, but if nobody will accept them or respond to them, you can call them leaders, but they are not leading. The thing that determines if a leader is leading is that the follower is following. So you've got to have two things in the structure: First you have to have leadership and secondly, you've got to have followership. This followership is made up of those prepared to be part of a group, who will so commit themselves to a group, and find nurture and care in that situation, that you don't have 2 million individuals saying, "I want to see Moses, and if I can't see Moses, I won't see anybody." There will be people who will be satisfied with being part of ten who are committed to each other, with somebody caring for them. If the one who is caring for the ten can't cope, then there is always the person who is handling fifty and they can refer to him. But the key is to get leadership that is prepared to be responsible and followers who will be responsive to following. Otherwise, it's hopeless.

Well, that's the structure. But you can put structure in place and still have nothing that works. I have seen all kinds of wonderful schemes and plans drawn up on computers in full color, with graphs and pies sliced up, flow charts that look like the Manhattan skyline, little boxes, lines and arrows that are superb. But in and of themselves, structures achieve little. The people of God are, and always have been, a living organism, not just an organization. Granted, living organisms have built-in organizations, but not all organizations become living organisms. It's the LIFE that makes the difference. You need the structure, but you've got to have life—the life of the Spirit.

The Spirit that had rested on Moses now rested on all these leaders. Moses could have been threatened by this, but he wasn't at all put out. In fact, when somebody came along claiming that some men were apparently ministering without Moses' permission, Joshua, his righthand man said, "Moses, my lord, stop them." But Moses replied, " . . . I wish that all the Lord's people were prophets and that the Lord would put His Spirit on them" (Numbers 11:29).

The structure was in place, the leaders were identified, the people were prepared to be part of the groups committed to followership, and the Spirit of God came upon them. Jethro had stipulated that the leaders should have *integrity* — they must not accept bribes, and *intensity* — they were to fear the Lord. When you have leaders of spiritual integrity and intensity, and the Holy Ghost falls upon them, you've got great leaders and people tend to follow them. Jethro's solution was simple but not easy, obvious but not superficial. It held great promise, but required great commitment.

Recently I read a very interesting document drawn up by the parishioners of the Roman Catholic Archdiocese of Victoria, Brazil. It was a statement about the kind of church they would like to see developed. Among other things it said, "We would like to see a church in which everybody feels they are really somebody — where everyone has a name and a face." I like that! But how do you do it? Well if Moses could do it with 2 million people, perhaps his way is worth trying!

The Complexity of the Procedure — Getting People to Care and Share

But things don't always work the way they are supposed to! You can have total simplicity of procedure and yet utter complexity when you try to make it work. The problem is getting people to care and to share. You see, if you're going to start caring, that's going to require change. This means challenge, and a reorganization of priorities. It means that you don't quite have the freedom to do things your own way; now you're committed to somebody else and they are committed to you. It means that when you are hurting, you are prepared to admit you're hurting and seek help. And it means that when you are healthy, you are prepared to channel your spiritual health into the lives of those who are hurting.

Let me ask you a question: are you hurting right now? Do you have a support group of caring, sharing, praying believers to whom you have been committed for a long time, so that as you began hurting you already had a support structure in place, so that you are being cared for? Or are you one of those people who have been on the edge? Things have been going from bad to worse and now you're in an impossible situation; you've no support group, nobody knows your name, nobody knows your face, nobody knows you well enough to really care for you and share with you, and you've suddenly gone to the leadership and said, "Here's my problem, solve it!"

Those of you who are healthy, who are living your own lives, not identifying with a group, not identifying with caring people, or sharing with other people, let me address some questions to you. Do you believe that when the Bible says it is more blessed to give than to receive that that is true? What evidence is there that you believe it? Do you believe what the Bible says about those who serve being "great"? What evidence is there? When the Bible says that a cup of cold water given in the name of Christ has immense value, do you believe that? What evidence is there that you believe it? One of the earliest questions ever asked was, "Am I my brother's keeper?" What is your answer?

A little over twenty years ago, there was a pastor in a struggling church in Korea. He had tuberculosis that was exacerbated by ulcers, and he was so overwhelmed by what he was trying to do in his ministry, and by his ill health, that he had a nervous breakdown. He decided that he just couldn't cope, much like Moses, and he told his congregation so. He suggested that the congregation should start caring for each other, that they should form a ministering network. He asked his leadership to help and the men said, "No." So he did something that was totally contrary to Korean culture; he turned to the women and they said, "Yes, we'll do it." And so the women began to establish caring, sharing groups throughout his little congregation. When he went off to the hospital, those women began to care, share, and reach out, and their caring and sharing attracted other people and the church began to grow. Now, the Full Gospel Church of Seoul, Korea, which in the early 1960s was a tiny church with a sick pastor, has in excess of 150,000 members. They have an auditorium that seats 10,000 with an overflow room with TV for 15,000. They have six services every Sunday. They have 10,000 small groups. They meet for prayer early in the morning or at the lunch hour in their place of work. Many of the people spend part of their vacation at a church-owned retreat center—a mountain full of caves where the people fast and pray. Pastor Cho has told the congregation that the armed divisions of North Korea are poised just twenty-six kilometers to the north and that if they come down, the first thing they will do is put him in jail. But the church will continue to grow because, like Moses, he has learned to share the burden and the people have learned to bear it.

If we are to enjoy the good life, God's way, we need to be part of a caring, sharing community of believers.

A nd now, O Israel, what does the Lord your God ask of you but to fear the Lord your God, to walk in all His ways, to love Him, to serve the Lord your God with all your heart and with all your soul, and to observe the Lord's commands and decrees that I am giving you today for your own good?

"To the Lord your God belong the heavens, even the highest heavens, the earth and everything in it. Yet the Lord set His affection on your forefathers and loved them, and He chose you, their descendants, above all the nations, as it is today. Circumcise your hearts, therefore, and do not be stiff-necked any longer. For the Lord your God is God of gods and Lord of lords, the great God, mighty and awesome, who shows no partiality and accepts no bribes.

"He defends the cause of the fatherless and the widow, and loves the alien, giving him food and clothing. And you are to love those who are aliens, for you yourselves were aliens in Egypt. Fear the Lord your God and serve Him. Hold fast to Him and take your oaths in His name. He is your praise; he is your God, who performed for you those great and awesome wonders you saw with your own eyes. Your forefathers who went down into Egypt were seventy in all, and now the Lord your God has made you as numerous as the stars in the sky."

Deuteronomy 10:12-22

THE HEART AND SOUL OF
THE GOOD LIFE

4 We all have certain expectations of God. Every time we pray, we articulate some of these expectations. We bring our petitions to Him; not infrequently we bring our objections and our complaints, and we expect Him to do something about them. We have certain expectations in terms of blessing and in terms of direction. We do, however, need to remember that God has very clearcut expectations of us.

We tend to think that if we could get our expectations of God met, that would be to our benefit. But in actual fact, Moses taught the people that they would derive greater benefit from meeting God's expectations, than from His meeting theirs. The divine expectations were for their own good (Deuteronomy 10:13).

The Priority

With that in mind, let's look at God's expectations. The Lord's primary expectation of us is that we should love Him. Granted, this expectation is in the middle of Moses' list: "And now, O Israel, what does the Lord your God ask of you but to fear the Lord your God, to walk in all His ways, to love

47

Him, to serve the Lord your God with all your heart and with all your soul, and to observe the Lord's commands and decrees that I am giving you today for your own good?" (10:12-13) But I want you to notice that God's expectation that we will love Him is repeated often in Deuteronomy.

Hear, O Israel: The Lord our God, the Lord is one. Love the Lord your God with all your heart and with all your soul and with all your strength (6:4-5).

Love the Lord your God and keep His requirements, His decrees, His laws and His commands always (11:1).

So if you faithfully obey the commands I am giving you today — to love the Lord your God and to serve Him with all your heart and with all your soul — then I will send rain on your land in its season (11:13).

If you carefully observe all these commands I am giving you to follow — to love the Lord your God, to walk in all His ways and to hold fast to Him — then the Lord will drive out all these nations before you (11:22).

The Lord your God is testing you to find out whether you love Him with all your heart and with all your soul (13:3).

Clearly the expectation that we will love our Lord is a priority. And it is not just an Old Testament concept. On one occasion an expert in the law came to Jesus. Testing Him with questions, he asked Him, "What is the greatest commandment?" And the Lord Jesus answered, "Love the Lord your God with all your heart and with all your soul and with all your mind" (Matthew 22:36-37).

• Clearly this is a *spiritual priority*. When you look at your spiritual life, you ought to be able to see at its core a deep love for the Lord. Now, of course, there are aids to spirituality. The Bible, prayer, the fellowship of believers, preaching and teaching, the music, all these things are intended to help the developing of your spiritual relationship. Unfortunately, it is sometimes possible for these aids to become more important than the Lord Himself. It is possible to love the church or the choir, the preaching or the preacher, more than you love the Lord. The tragedy of this is that things and people can disappoint you. Not infrequently, in church life you will find that people become disappointed with the choir or the music or the preacher or the fellowship or the structure or the facilities, and then drop out. The one thing that will hold you firm, even when you are disappointed, is to love the Lord most of all.

● On one occasion where the Lord Jesus was addressing His disciples on the subject of discipleship, He said to them, "Anyone who loves his father or mother more than Me is not worthy of Me; anyone who loves his son or daughter more than Me is not worthy of Me" (Matthew 10:37). This is a reminder that the top *relational priority* is to love the Lord our God. This does not mean that we should not love our father and mother, our sons and daughters. But there may come a time when we have to decide on the top priority in our life — whether it is the Lord or our family, the Lord or our friends. At that time, the disciple will put the Lord first. This is a very hard saying that does not in any way diminish the importance of friends or family; it simply points out to us that unless we love the Lord first, we are not going to have the ability to love our friends and family appropriately. Both the spiritual priority and the relational priority is "loving the Lord your God."

● Then there is the *motivational priority*. The Apostle Paul wrote to the Corinthians, a greatly gifted congregation who were using their wonderful gifts in all kinds of exotic and esoteric ways, and pointed out to them that they should not become so enamored with their gifts and their capabilities that they overlooked the motivational priority in their lives. He said, in effect, "If I speak in the tongues of men and of angels but have not love, if I give my body to be burned, if I give everything I possess to the poor and have not love, I'm as empty as a sounding brass, I'm as meaningless as a tinkling triangle, I am nothing and I have nothing." In other words, it is possible for me to engage in all kinds of charitable activities and sacrificial service; but if my motivation is not a genuine love for the Lord, there is something singularly lacking. Our relationships, our spirituality, our motivation must all be governed by the Lord Himself, and by our love for Him. He is to be Number One in our hearts. That's the expectation He has of us and it is for *our* good—not His!

The Reality

As soon as we say we are supposed to love God, we run into problems. *How* do we love God? Do we love God they way we love a girlfriend, a wife or a family? Do we love God the way we love a job, hunting and fishing, or a Golden Retriever? How do we love God? There is considerable confusion on this point, but there is also clear amplification, because Moses told the people, "Love the Lord your God with all your heart and with all your soul and with all your strength" (6:5). Now these three words, *heart, soul* and *strength* are not window dressing. They show us in very practical terms the reality of love.

• Heart reality. In this context the heart suggests the mind-set. Our lives to a very large extent are governed by our mind-set—whatever in our minds is of primary importance. And God is concerned that we should have a mind-set that places God and love for Him as central. This is particularly important, because there is a tendency for us to be external in our religion and superficial in our spirituality. What God is looking for is internal reality.

Moses said to the people, "Circumcise your hearts, therefore, and do not be stiff-necked any longer" (10:16). Loving with the heart requires circumcision of the heart. I know that's a strange expression, but let me remind you that God had made a covenant with His people. The sign of the covenant, the evidence that humans were participating in it, was that Abraham and his male descendants were physically circumcised. This was the outward and visible sign of an inward and spiritual reality. Now then, God was saying that it was possible to go through all kinds of outward and physical external signs or activities that were not related to inward, spiritual realities. Or, to put it in simpler terms, it was possible for the people of Israel to be externally circumcised and to say, "We're members of the covenant people," but not to have their minds and hearts set on being the covenant people.

We have our ecclesiastical rituals today and they can be devoid of reality. You don't need to be very smart, very strong, or very holy to take a piece of bread and a little cup of wine, and eat and drink with a sober expression on your face. But the act can be purely external, purely formal, and utterly superficial. If I take the bread and eat it, I am really saying, "Inwardly, spiritually, I am feeding on Christ; He is the staple diet of my spiritual life." And if I drink the wine, what I am really saying is, "This speaks of His blood shed for me, and as I partake of it I am making a statement of the fact that the blood of Christ, His death on the cross, alone satisfies for sin, and alone sets me free from the power of sin." But I can take the bread and wine without any sense of reality at all. If I do that, I need to circumcise my heart, to have my mind set on the fact that Christ is the staple diet of my life and that it is Christ's death alone which meets my deepest needs. If that is not the case, a lot of junk needs to be cleared out of my heart, out of my mind-set. I need a reorientation, or as Paul would put it, I need to have my "mind renewed." When that happens I can begin to have my mind set on loving the Lord.

There are a couple of references in Deuteronomy to God testing us to see what is in our hearts. "Remember how the Lord your God led you all the way in the desert forty years, to humble you and to test you in order to know what was in your heart, whether or not you would keep His commands" (8:2). God allows tests to come our way in order that He might see what is going on inside our hearts. In the movie *Fatal Attraction,* the character played by Michael Douglas is "happily married" — lovely wife and beautiful child, good job, magnificent home. The "good life" according to many. The wife and child go away for the weekend, but he has a business appointment. He goes to the appointment and meets the character played by Glenn Close. She makes it very clear that she is attracted to him, that she is available, and then she aggressively pursues him. This is a major test that shows what's in his heart. Is deep love, faithfulness, and commitment to his wife and to his child and family his mind-set? No. The pressure he comes under is such that he and we discover what is in his heart. He is fundamentally adulterous, but it takes a test to prove what is potentially or actually there. Now God is so anxious for us to discover whether our fundamental mind-set is commitment and love to Him, that He will allow the tests to come so that we know what is in our hearts.

The second test is to find out whether we love Him with all our heart and soul and strength. "The Lord your God is testing you to find out whether you love Him with all your heart and with all your soul" (Deuteronomy 13:3). When I was a teenager, a Captain in the Royal Artillery marched into my life. I was particularly bored in the little church in which I was brought up, and he was like a breath of fresh air. It was during World War II and he became part of our family. I kept in touch with him until he died at the age of ninety-one. Shortly before he died he achieved his lifetime ambition — he was personally presented to Her Majesty the Queen. He sprang to attention out of his wheelchair and stood there briefly, bowed, and then collapsed into his wheelchair again.

When I was joining the Marines he told me, "Stuart, the first night in the Marines you will nail your colors to the mast." It was interesting that he, an Army man, should use a Naval expression. For the benefit of those who are not familiar with Naval traditions, let me explain. In the old days when a ship surrendered, someone would haul down the colors. But on some ships to make absolutely certain that nobody would haul down the colors from the masthead, they would actually nail the colors to the mast, as they sailed into battle. This meant, "No surrender under any circumstances."

I said, "How do I nail my colors to the mast the first night in the Marines?"

He replied, "You go into the barrack room and at the appropriate time you will kneel by your bed and you'll pray."

I said, "What will happen?"

"All kinds of things could happen. They will probably throw boots at you. If they do, you clean them, and you return them the next morning. But you will nail your colors to the mast."

Well, when I walked into that barrack roomful of Marine recruits, I realized that they were not the sweetest, gentlest people I had ever seen in my life, and the thought of kneeling down by my bed to pray in full view of them was most daunting. God put me to the test and it was simply this, "Do you love Me more or do you fear them more? Show Me." Well, of course, you know that I did what I was supposed to do; otherwise I would have thought of another illustration! I knelt down, but hoped they wouldn't notice me. There was total silence and I realized everybody had seen me. Then worse, the floor boards creaked and I realized they were all walking toward me and gathering around the bed. I couldn't think of a thing to pray, so I counted up to twenty-five and got up. I felt desperately foolish, but deep in my heart I don't think I've ever been more thrilled. By that simple action I had said, "I love You, Lord, and I don't care what they do."

• Soul reality. If heart love has to do with mind-set, soul love has to do with emotion, with intensity. People can do music different ways. Some get up and sing and they get all the notes just right. Other people sing and there is a grip, an intensity about it. It's called "soul," a thing as indefinable as it is undeniable. Some singers put you to sleep, while others get you on your feet. Intensity, emotion, soul.

One day Jesus asked a very powerful question, "What shall a man give in exchange for his soul?" He meant, "What will a man give in exchange for the whole of his life? What is it that makes him tick? What is he essentially, emotionally, intensely? What is he when push comes to shove?" Paul said, "For me to live is Christ." That's soul intensity. In marked contrast to that I watched an interview with Vanna White who appears on a show called "Wheel of Fortune" in which people guess individual letters. When they guess right, Vanna claps, smiles, and displays the letter! She is a beautiful girl and the interviewer asked her if she was going to go into movies. She said, "Probably not, because I have a contract up to 1992 with "Wheel of Fortune." But then she said something with a radiant smile that I found desperately sad. She said, "Turning letters is my life."

What's your life? Fill in the blank. "_____ is my life." What you write is your emotional intensity. That part of you is supposed to be channeled into love for the Lord — "with all your soul."

• Strength reality. I don't understand the mechanics of falling in love, but I know what it feels like, since I did it. Young people who fall in love want to get married and live happily ever after. But you can't have a marriage based just on the feelings of falling in love. There comes a time when that initial attraction, whatever it is, has to be solidified by commitment. Then having solidified the initial attraction by commitment, you spend the next thirty, forty, or fifty years, depending on how long the Lord graciously gives you, ratifying that commitment. The commitment is an act of will, the ratification is an act of will, and it's all a demonstration of love. This is the idea behind loving God with all our strength. It's a matter of the will, of commitment. Whatever the initial attraction to Him may have been, whatever the miracle that brought us to the point of being in love with Him, the initial attraction has to be solidified by commitment and that commitment has to be ratified by acts of the will perpetually demonstrating, "I love You with all my heart, with all my soul, and with all my strength." The language of life becomes, "Lord, my mind is set, my emotions are intense, my will is settled. You're my Lord." That's His expectation of us. So to summarize, His expectation is that we give Him an intelligent, enthusiastic, practical response to His loving initiative in our lives. That's what He expects and it's for our good!

To Know Him Is to Love Him

Some immediate questions come to mind. "How in the world do I ever get myself into that frame of mind? How do I ever start to feel that emotional intensity? With all the other things that challenge me to make decisions, how do I decide with my will?" Good and important questions. The answer that comes through loudly and clearly is you love Him in direct proportion to your knowledge of Him. Or to put it colloquially, "To know Him is to love Him." If you find that your love is weak and frail, it is highly likely that your knowledge of Him is superficial and deficient. Notice how this passage goes on to explain who He is. He is identified as the *God of creation.* "To the Lord your God belong the heavens, even the highest heavens, the earth and everything in it" (10:14). Do you believe that? Do you believe that by His creative rights everything belongs to Him, including you and all that belongs to you? If you are grateful for everything that belongs to you, to whom are you grateful? Are you grateful to the God of creation who made it and to whom it ultimately belongs? If so, how you must love Him! You look at your home and all that belongs to you. You look around at your family and all that belongs to you. You look in your closet, you go in your garage, you go to your work, you check your bankbook and your investments, and how you love Him! For He created all that you have and it belongs to Him. To know Him as the great Creator is to love Him.

Of course, some people think of the Creator as a mechanistic device, impersonally churning out creations. But this is inappropriate because He is the *God of affection*. Having made this great statement about the Lord, Moses immediately added, "Yet the Lord set His affection on your forefathers and loved them" (10:15). You always find this balance in Scripture. On the one hand, the transcendent glory of His creative majesty and on the other, His immanent warmth, concern, and affection for us. But the balance must be maintained.

Moses went on to say, "The Lord your God is God of gods and Lord of lords, the great God, mighty and awesome who shows no partiality and accepts no bribes" (10:17). He is the *God of perfection*. Incredibly He cares for the oppressed; as Moses explained, "He defends the cause of the fatherless and the widow, and loves the alien, giving him food and clothing (10:18), proving He is the *God of compassion*. No wonder Moses exclaimed, "He is your praise," for He is the *God of adoration*. No recital of God's intervention on the part of the Children of Israel is ever complete without mention of His saving acts, His "great and awesome wonders" (12:21) which then, as now, remind God's people that He is the *God of salvation*. The extent to which we know Him in these dimensions will determine to a very large extent the depth of our love for Him.

I loved my mother just because she was my mother. But as I was growing up, I discovered one day that she had almost died giving birth to me, and when I heard that I felt a new quality of love for her. When my brother and I were kids, she had super high blood pressure and my father had been drafted during World War II. She ran the family business with two small kids to look after and felt dreadful most days. When I was a teenager, she was diagnosed as having cancer and I realized something of the intense pain that she was suffering. She never grumbled, the business grew, we were raised and we recognized a great lady. To know her was to love her. Eventually when my grandmother was dying, my mother said, "Your grandmother looked after me when I was helpless; I will look after her while she is helpless." The doctors warned her that it was too much for her, but she did it anyway. One day she was found unconscious in her chair, having suffered a massive coronary with nobody around except her invalid mother. When I heard that about her, I loved her even more. To know her was to love her. The more I discovered the deeper aspects of her character, the more I was stimulated to deeper response in my heart. There was an instinctual love first, but then it was educated. And that's how it is with God. We are to meditate upon Him. We are to concentrate upon Him. We are to be educated about Him. We are to assimilate what we know of Him. Then we will know Him, and to know Him will be to love Him.

At the beginning of this chapter, we noted a list of divine expectations that center on loving the Lord our God. But what are these other requirements? To fear, to walk, to serve, to observe. All, of course, are related to love for Him. Any or all of these things, divorced from a glad response to His grace, becomes a dead, debilitating exercise. All of these things based on love become the means to enjoying the good life.

The fear of God is a very unpopular topic at the present time. Recently, Jill and I were speaking at a Pastors and Spouses Conference, and during a question time we were asked a number of questions on the theme, "Do you really feel that we are supposed to fear God?" Interesting, isn't it? I would suggest that the idea of fearing God, of having a tremendous sense of His awesome holiness, and of coming before

Him with the degree of humility and solemnity that is appropriate to His holiness, is somewhat foreign to us. Part of the reason is that in our modern world we pride ourselves in discovering a naturalistic, scientific explanation for almost everything, which means that the supernatural, awesome power of God is something we don't think about too much! Many years ago a German student was walking on a road and lightning struck him and he was felled to the ground. His response was to cry at the top of his voice in absolute terror, "St. Anne, save me and I will become a monk." His response, in the context of the religion he understood at that time, was to sense that God in His awesome power had intervened in his life through that lightning, and he committed himself to become a monk. That student, Martin Luther, changed the course of Europe and of the church.

At the Western Open in Chicago a few years ago, Lee Trevino and two other professional golfers were on the fairway when a storm came up and lightning struck them. In an interview shortly after, Trevino was asked what lessons he had learned from this horrendous experience. He said, "I learned that if the Almighty wants to play through, you let Him; and I decided that in a lightning storm in the future, I would hold a one iron above my head." When asked, "Why a one iron?" he said, "Because even God can't hit a one iron!" You'll get one man struck by lightning who responded with a sense of the awesome power of God and is humbled in service. The other man jokes about it. Of course, I know nothing of Mr. Trevino's heart relationship to the Lord, but his response to lightning was certainly poles apart from Luther's reaction.

If we are to take seriously what it means to know and love God, we will learn to fear Him, to reverence His majesty, to follow His leading, to serve His cause, to obey His commands, to love His people, to practice His presence, and to worship His name. In other words, the recipe for the good life is not to make demands of God, but rather to meet the divine expectations. They are overwhelming; but fortunately, we have the death of Christ to touch our hearts and to cleanse our sins, and we have the Spirit of God to spur us on in His power.

Let me ask you four questions. What is your mind-set? What is your emotional intensity? What do you will to do? Is it to love God?

Moses summoned all Israel and said, "Hear, O Israel, the decrees and laws I declare in your hearing today. Learn them and be sure to follow them. The Lord our God made a covenant with us at Horeb. It was not with our fathers that the Lord made this covenant, but with us, with all of us who are alive here today. The Lord spoke to you face to face out of the fire on the mountain. (At that time I stood between the Lord and you to declare to you the word of the Lord, because you were afraid of the fire and did not go up the mountain.) And He said:

" 'I am the Lord your God, who brought you out of Egypt, out of the land of slavery. You shall have no other gods before Me.

" 'You shall not make for yourself an idol in the form of anything in heaven above or on the earth beneath or in the waters below. You shall not bow down to them or worship them; for I, the Lord your God, am a jealous God, punishing the children for the sin of the fathers to the third and fourth generation of those who hate Me, but showing love to a thousand generations of those who love Me and keep My commandments.

" 'You shall not misuse the name of the Lord your God, for the Lord will not hold anyone guiltless who misuses His name.

" 'Observe the Sabbath day by keeping it holy, as the Lord your God has commanded you. Six days you shall labor and do all your work, but the seventh day is a Sabbath to the Lord your God. On it you shall not do any work, neither you, nor your son or daughter, nor your manservant or maidservant, nor your ox, your donkey, or any of your animals, nor the alien within your gates, so that your manservant and maidservant may rest, as you do. Remember that you were slaves in Egypt and that the Lord your God brought you out of there with a mighty hand and an outstretched arm. Therefore the Lord your God has commanded you to observe the Sabbath day.' "

Deuteronomy 5:1-15

SPIRITUAL VALUES
OF THE GOOD LIFE

5 Presidential candidates and other seekers-of-office carefully enumerate the issues on which they disagree. But occasionally they discover issues on which they are in agreement. Recently, one of these has been "traditional family values." Candidates arrange photo opportunities with their children and their in-laws and their grandchildren, not to mention family pets. Presumably, the conventional wisdom is that "traditional family values" score well with the majority of the voting public.

If ever you attend a party where the conversation is lagging, just interject the subject of "the public school system." Immediately things will perk up considerably! Then if you use some highly emotional phrases like "value clarifications" or "value-neutral education," you will really get folks going. The introduction of "value clarifications" into the school curriculum is, as I understand it, an attempt to help young people to decide what is good, better, and best, and what is bad, worse, and worst. On the other hand, "value neutralists" seem to want to avoid any such approach. It seems to me that "value clarification" and "value neutrality" need clarification. But "values" are big. The "V" word is on many lips.

James Reichley, a senior fellow at the Brookings Institute, in his book, *Religion in American Public Life*, wrote that religion and politics have one thing in common: they both seek after values. But because they frequently seek different values, they are headed on a collision course. He wrote, "What democracy needs is a value system that legitimatizes both individual rights and social authority and establishes a balance between the two."[1] He explained that some people base their values on "individual rights." Of course, to insist on individual rights to the exclusion of everything else will produce anarchy, not society. On the other hand, there are people who say we must concentrate on "social authority" to produce a value system which will show us the way to go. The problem, however, with unlimited social authority is that it can all too easily degenerate into a totalitarianism that abrogates human freedoms and human rights. So, what we need in our democracy is a value system "that legitimizes individual rights and social authority and establishes a balance between the two." But where in the world are we going to find such a system? And how are we all going to agree on it?

The Sources of Values

There are three possible sources of a value system. One is *personal*, as I look into myself and decide my personal values and how I'm going to live my life. If anybody suggests that my values are inadequate then I can tell them to get off my back and mind their own business, while I mind mine. The "free to be me" sort of thing.

Another source is the *society* round about me. It may be either a totalitarian regime which imposes its will upon me, or it may be a republican/democratic system where we elect representatives to pass laws and a president who appoints supreme court justices. These officials determine what our values will be.

The third approach is to base values on an authority separate from and greater than self and society—a *transcendental* source. Reichley states,

> A society that gives an important place to self-interest will tend to emphasize such values as personal freedom, individual initiative and gratification of the senses. A society that is more devoted to group interests will stress cooperation, discipline, obedience, continuity and social order. A society that is most concerned with transcendent purpose will attach particular value to piety, reverence, humility before God, and loving relationships.[2]

We all have a value system, even though we may not know it by such a grand name. The question is, "From whence does our personal value system come?" Does it come from our inherent sense of what we want? Do we simply go along with what society says? Or do we believe in a transcendent authority? These are profoundly important questions, particularly if we are interested in enjoying the good life.

If we had been part of Moses' congregation on the day he was teaching Deuteronomy 5, we might have gone to him and said, "Excuse me, Moses, but I need to feel free to be me." He probably would have said, "I'll have a little word with you later." Someone else might have said, "Moses, we don't like the way you are talking; we're going to start a recall action against you and put somebody else in your place. We'll elect a new leader who will go along with what the majority feels is best for us." His response might have been, "We don't operate around here on what the individual feels intrinsically or on what the society determines collectively. We work on the basis of a transcendent authority called the Lord our God."

The God of Values

The Bible has no introduction and no preamble and does not ease into its subject. It hits it head on. The very first phrase of the very first sentence of the very first chapter of the very first book says, "In the beginning God created. . . ." That is the fundamental premise of Scripture. It tells us that there is a ground of being from whom all things come, and upon whom all things are dependent and contingent. That is a basic premise of biblical revelation. Now if I accept that there is a transcendent authority, a God who is the ground of all being, and that everything — including me — is contingent upon Him and dependent upon Him, then clearly I have staked out the basis of my value system. It is the transcendent authority who created me.

However, it is rather obvious that there are people who do not accept the premise that God created them; therefore, they do not accept that they are contingent and dependent upon Him. This leaves them dependent on their own resources, individually or collectively. The result is a great divide between those who acknowledge a creative God by whom and through whom all things exist, and those who find their reason for being in themselves or in their society. So the decision we must make first is this: Is there or is there not a God who created, who is the transcendent authority? Moses was unequivocal on this point.

• Notice, however, that he was not talking about a God who only created, but about a God who also *cares*. This God of whom Moses spoke had seen His people in bondage in Egypt and was deeply disconcerted about their circumstances. God called Moses and said, "I have seen the anguish of My people, their cries have risen to Me, and I am going to send you to Pharaoh to say, 'Let My people go.' " The living God cares. You'll notice that caring in the preamble to the Ten Commandments where God said, "I am the Lord your God who brought you out of Egypt, out of the land of slavery." In other words, the Ten Commandments are predicated on the fact that the creative God is a caring God.

Now, the Israelites were suffering not solely from taskmaster bondage; they were also in bondage to a wilderness experience that was not imposed upon them by anybody but themselves. They were living with the consequences of their own wrong actions. But God cares, whether we suffer from "self-imposed" or "other imposed" bondage. Sometimes we suffer because of what people have done to us; other times we suffer because of what we have done to ourselves. But the same principle obtains — there is a God who cares and addresses the point of bondage and says, "Let My people go."

• He is also the God who *covenants*. This is a theme that recurs constantly. Moses reminded the people, "The Lord our God made a covenant with us at Horeb." The creative, caring God had personalized His interest in the people of Israel. He promised to be their God, to care for them, direct them and oversee their affairs, and provide all that they needed. He asked only for their allegiance in return. This covenant was the basis upon which the Ten Commandments were given. The expected response to the covenant-making God was that they would love Him with all their heart and all their soul and all their strength. Those are abstract concepts, and so God put the abstract in the concrete and said, "If you want to know how to love Me with all your heart, soul, and strength, here are ten ways to do it." And that's what the Ten Commandments are all about.

• He is a God who creates and who cares and who covenants, and who also *communicates* with His people. Moses said, "The Lord spoke to you face to face out of the fire on the mountain. At that time I stood between the Lord and you to declare to you the word of the Lord, because you were afraid of the fire and did not go up the mountain. It was not with our fathers that the Lord made this covenant, but with us" (5:4-5, 3). Most of the people Moses was talking to had been born in the wilderness during the last forty years, after the Commandments were delivered. The people who had originally received the Commandments were dead. But Moses said that it was to "us," those who were born after the event that he spoke of, not with their fathers. What was he saying? Perhaps his point was that "the God who communicated His principles in the past is still communicating them anew and afresh today." He who created us cares deeply for us, makes a covenant with us sealed with the blood of His Son, our Lord Jesus, continually communicates to us in order that we might know who He is and what He says, so that we might make an ongoing application of His value systems day by day.

● But He is also the God who *commands*. Notice the tone in which Moses spoke. "Hear, O Israel, the decrees and the laws I declare in your hearing today." Ted Koppel once said that God gave us Ten Commandments, not ten suggestions. There is an authoritative voice in the commandments of God. Authority resides in Him and He expects us to respect His authority in our daily lives, for in His authority is the source of all spiritual values. God wants to work in our lives in order that we may "live and prosper and prolong our days" (v. 33). Or to use our phrase, "in order that we might enjoy the good life."

The Spiritual Values
Let us now look at the substance of these spiritual values, outlined in the first half of the Ten Commandments.

● The *exclusiveness* of God. "You shall have no other gods before Me" is quite straightforward. God insists on exclusive rights to His people, and if this exclusive relationship is deeply embedded in their thinking, it becomes a solid base upon which value systems are built. When other things that are contrary to my God demand my allegiance, then the answer is "No!" This distinction was particularly necessary for the Children of Israel as they entered the Promised Land. They were traditionally nomads. When they went down into Egypt, they started raising sheep. The Egyptians hated sheep and detested shepherds, and so the Israelites started out on the wrong foot. But when they went into the Promised Land, they were going to be neither nomads nor shepherds, but farmers, and they didn't know anything about it. So how were they going to learn? Probably from the people who were already doing it — the Canaanites. The problem, however, was that the Canaanite approach to farming was forbidden to the Israelites. In the Canaanite agricultural system, fertility gods decided whether it would rain, whether the sun would shine, and whether there would be a good harvest. Because everything depended on the gods, the farmers had to ensure that their fertility gods were kept happy. How did they do that? By engaging in the aspect of their own lives that had to do with fertility. Yes, you guessed it — sex. Their system of farming required religious practices involving all kinds of sexual promiscuity. One wonders how they ever had time to farm! If the people of Israel went into the land of Caanan and started to farm that way, immediately the fertility gods would be brought in alongside Jehovah. Before it could even happen, God said, "Oh, no, you don't! Those fertility gods stand for everything that I stand against." The modern word for this kind of blend of belief is *syncretism;* God would not tolerate it then and He will not tolerate it now, particularly when syncretism leads to sensualism.

Is this applicable to us today? Of course, it is. Some people make a very tidy dichotomy between Sundays and weekdays. They don't ever let their Sundays interfere with their work; or, to put it another way, they never let church interfere with the marketplace. Why? Because there are gods of the marketplace and there is the God of the church; the God of Sunday and the gods of Monday through Saturday. They have a syncretistic religion in which they expect the principles and values of the gods of the marketplace to live cheek by jowl with the one true God, Jehovah, even though the gods of the marketplace are in diametric opposition at times to the God Jehovah. God says, "No, you don't. I insist on being the Lord your

God in the worship place and the workplace." That helps me to sharpen the focus of my value system. The exclusiveness of God!

● The *uniqueness* of God. God added, "You shall not make for yourself an idol in the form of anything in heaven above or on earth beneath or in the waters below" (v. 8). Man has always had the desire to try to figure out what God is like. We read in Scripture that in the beginning God created man in His own image. And ever since man has been trying to re-create God in his own image. Therein lies the problem. We all have a tendency to worship a god crafted with the materials of our own imagination, a god who fits conveniently into our own structures, making few demands and expecting only the changes we deem in our best interests. This is the essence of idolatry. It doesn't mean that we bow down to a little clay thing and burn incense before a god-shelf in the den. It means that we are substituting something of our own creation for God. This, of course, must, by definition, be utterly inadequate. The uniqueness of God can never be expressed by anything man makes or initiates. Idols substitute the created for the Creator. Clearly they cannot demonstrate the uniqueness of God. Idols substitute human imagination about God for divine revelation of who God is. Idols substitute human limitations and understanding of God for the illimitable transcendence of God. Idols substitute man's superiority over God for human submission to God.

Living as we do in a pluralistic society, it is relatively easy to see how we can have other gods. We rejoice in our freedoms; we rejoice in the fact that our democracy allows us to believe fervently what we wish to believe. But we have to recognize that democracy inevitably produces pluralism and pluralism inevitably spawns all kinds of value systems which, in turn, create all manner of conflict and confusion. In our society everybody has the right to believe what they wish, to challenge anybody who believes differently, and to insist on the right to propagate their own point of view. This kind of freedom has many pluses and minuses. The up-side is that true spiritual values can be shared freely. The down-side is that the false values can claim at least equal time.

We rejoice in our freedom of religion, but freedom of religion presupposes freedom for irreligion too. So if we have a mandated freedom for irreligion which we cherish because we cherish freedom of religion, and we can't have the one without the other, then we've got to accept that there will be irreligion that challenges what we believe at every point. Alongside God will be many gods, and if we're not careful the gods may win the battle for men's hearts and minds. Our value systems must be based on the exclusiveness and the uniqueness of God.

● The *righteousness* of God. One of the most troubling passages of Scripture is, "For I, the Lord your God am a jealous God punishing the children for the sin of the fathers to the third and fourth generation of those who hate Me, but showing love to a thousand generations of those who love Me and keep My commandments" (vv. 9-10). The picture of a jealous God punishing innocent children is less than appealing. But we must be careful. When God is described as "jealous," we must not imagine a "green-eyed" God. For "jealous," read "zealous." "White-hot intensity"—that's the meaning of "jealous" here. God feels intensely about righteousness or "rightness." He is jealous for righteousness. He is zealous with a white-hot intensity that things be right.

One of the things that He feels is absolutely right is that man should be free. He recognizes that man in his freedom chooses to sin, but He believes that man should be free to sin and free to live with the consequences of his sin. The tragedy, however, is that people who are free to sin and free to live with the consequences of sin, impose the consequences of their sin on the first, second, third, and fourth generations. If you drop a pebble in a pool you start ripples, and it is much easier to start them than to stop them. When you sin, you cannot stop the ramifications. God says it is right that you should be free to behave rightly, and it is right that you should be free not to behave rightly; but it is also right that you live with the consequences of your unrighteousness. The tragedy is the impact on society. Notice also that God's commitment to righteousness requires that He move in love toward those who are victimized. In so doing, He breaks the cycle, and arrests the ripples.

A couple confided in me recently that they were the third and fourth generation of adult children of alcoholics. They described how this had impacted their lives, and the problems that they had been experiencing in their marriage and with their children. Then they said, "But God has touched our hearts and has drawn us to Himself. He has been teaching us new principles, and in His grace and mercy He has broken the cycle." While God's commitment to righteousness has dire consequences for the unrepentant, it offers untold help and blessing to those who respond to His grace. This profoundly impacts our personal values. How else could it be, since we believe in the uniqueness and the exclusiveness and the righteousness of God?

● The *holiness* of God. "You shall not misuse the name of the Lord your God." This means much more than "you shouldn't cuss, swear, or blaspheme." It is saying, in effect, that when God revealed His name, He revealed His character. To "misuse" His name is to "abuse" His character and to besmirch His honor. Nobody better besmirch His honor! There is an awesomeness and a holiness about God which calls for deep honor and respect. Those who love Him are concerned that all that He stands for might be seen as "hallowed" and "holy." So they pray, "Hallowed be Thy name."

● The *pervasiveness* of God. When God talks about the Sabbath Day He says, "Six days shall you labor." He insists on telling you how to work. "On the seventh day," He says, "you shall rest," which means He insists on talking about your leisure. He also says that on the Sabbath Day you are to "remember" that you were delivered from your bondage. Here He is talking about worship. He also says that you are to give other people a chance to rest. Here He is talking about your relationships. Now what else is your life but work, leisure, worship, and relationships?

God pervades every dimension of life, and in so doing presents us with a fascinating value system. When we pull all these things together, we ask ourselves, "What is the significance of these spiritual values?" The answer is very simple. They determine the kind of people we are and, accordingly, they determine the way we live. In the midst of all the talk about values clarification and the debate about value-free education and discussion of traditional family values, there is a pressing need for solid spiritual values. We need to believe that there is a transcendent value system, and then need to ensure that we are consistently living by it. This is the way to discover and enjoy the good life.

Honor your father and your mother, as the Lord your God has commanded you, so that you may live long and that it may go well with you in the land the Lord your God is giving you.

"You shall not murder.

"You shall not commit adultery.

"You shall not steal.

"You shall not give false testimony against your neighbor.

"You shall not covet your neighbor's wife. You shall not set your desire on your neighbor's house or land, his manservant or maidservant, his ox or donkey, or anything that belongs to your neighbor."

Deuteronomy 5:16-21

SOCIAL VALUES
OF THE GOOD LIFE

6 The first four of the Ten Commandments show that it is imperative that we build our lives on fundamental, spiritual values. Their focus is, "I am the Lord your God." God reminded His people that He was "the Lord your God who brought you out of Egypt, out of the land of slavery." The Lord our God who is the focus of our values is the One who took the initiative and brought redemption to us, offered Himself to us in a glorious covenant, and now asks that we respond to Him in loving, reverent obedience. That is the basis on which we are to live. The great and glorious Creator has made a covenant of redemption with us and makes available to us all that we need for this life and the life to come, and He asks only for our grateful response of love. This is summarized in the words, "Love the Lord your God with all your heart and with all your soul and with all your strength" (6:5).

However, we don't live in isolation. We live in society and in relationships. To a very large extent, the reality of our spiritual values is demonstrated in the quality of our social values. What we believe about God is shown very clearly in the way we treat people. That is why the six commands we look at in this chapter deal with social values. Those values are summarized in the instruction, "Love your neighbor as yourself." When the Lord Jesus was asked about the greatest commandment He said without hesitation, " 'Love the Lord your God with all your heart and with all your soul and all your mind.' This is the first and greatest commandment. And the second is like it: 'Love your neighbor as yourself' " (Matthew 22:37-39). The spiritual values and social values upon which our lives are built are bound up in each other.

Honor Your Father and Mother

The fifth commandment required, "Honor your father and your mother, as the Lord your God has commanded you." This reminds us that social values are learned in the family. The Lord gave two reasons for making "parent honoring" the solid foundation of family living. The first is "so that you may live long," and the second, "that it may go well with you in the land your God is giving you."

● "That you may live long" addressed the issue of *economic survival.* The people of Israel were about to go into a land where they would embark on a new lifestyle. They were going to engage in agriculture — something for which they had no training or experience; also, they were going to be surrounded by enemies. Their position was precarious in the extreme. But the one who had become their covenant God had promised to fight on their behalf, caring, protecting and providing, if they would maintain the covenant and follow a loving, obedient, reverent lifestyle. But succeeding generations would need to learn this also, and the family was to be their university, with father and mother as tenured professors, living in an honorable and exemplary manner. You'll remember that the second commandment stated, "You shall not make for yourself an idol," and God explained that the result of breaking this command would be that their idolatry would reverberate down to third and fourth generations. On the other hand, if the people would love and honor Him, then He would act on their behalf and show mercy and grace to thousands of people with even greater reverberations. Parental responsibility in the matrix of the family included adherence to the covenant by way of *example,* and teaching of the covenant by way of *instruction.* But failure to do this would result in negative impact down to the third and fourth generations. Parental sin would find a lodging place in the lives of their children. However, if the parents recognized what they had done and turned again to the covenant Lord, then He would show grace and mercy, which would positively impact the following generations. What a responsibility on the parents! What an opportunity for the family! What a tragedy when people fail to recognize the family as the place where social values are learned.

• The result of "honoring father and mother" was that it might "go well with you in the land the Lord your God is giving you." We have invented a word recently that never sounds right to me, but I use it anyway; the word is *wellness.* It means more than physical health, more than not being sick. Wellness has something to do with emotional stability and all-round health. We are integrated people. Spirit, soul and body interrelate in health or disease; and if one part is sick, then other parts of our being are affected. That is why when we counsel with people, we have to be careful to find out whether we are dealing with a spiritual problem, a physical problem, or a psychological problem. A spiritual problem may produce emotional imbalance; an emotional disorder will often produce physiological symptoms, and physical illness can create emotional and spiritual havoc. God told His people, "If it is going to go well with you," or to use our contemporary expression, "If it's wellness you want, the family is the place where you learn and teach integrated living."

• There is a third factor that we must note. Social values are for *economic survival,* for *emotional stability,* and also to establish an *educational structure.* You'll notice as we work through the social values in the Ten Commandments, we see that they all relate to self-interest in its proper place, and "proper place" is the operative phrase. In the Commandments, loving one's neighbor is related to loving oneself. This does not mean, as some contemporary teachers suggest, that there are three love commandments — love God, love neighbor, love self. Granted, many people have been so abused that their self-image is damaged and their self-esteem is deficient, and they undoubtedly need help and encouragement. But this does not give us the freedom to say that God commands us to love ourselves. He assumes we will, even if our self-image and self-esteem are less than ideal.

The assumption of Scripture is that everybody, however damaged, has a degree of self-love built into their psyche. They have a desire for acceptance, a longing for respect, an ache to be taken seriously, and a need to matter. They resent being disregarded, and they feel cheated if their rights — real or imagined — are not honored. They look earnestly for ways in which their "felt needs" can be satisfied, the inner longings of their souls assuaged.

This is the "self-love" which to a greater or lesser extent is evidenced in everyone. It is not necessary to command it. It is only necessary to acknowledge it, and then to channel the same kind of love to neighbors — and that certainly has to be commanded! I think we could probably say that one of the root problems in modern society is not a deficiency of self-interest or self-love, but an excess. If we are to learn the proper place of self-interest, we're going to need help, because self-interest so easily gives way to self-gratification, and self-gratification readily succumbs to excess, and excess inevitably leads to personal destruction and societal disintegration.

Somewhere along the line, we've got to build in that good old Christian principle of self-denial of which we hear so little today. Self-assertiveness, self-awareness, self-improvement are propagated by preachers and pop-psychologists with great fervor; but we must recognize that if we are to live wisely and well in society, then self-denial must be an intricate part of our lifestyle. Where do we learn this? In the matrix of the family.

Do Not Wrong Your Neighbor

Now we move into a consideration of the next four commandments: "You shall not murder, You shall not commit adultery, You shall not steal, You shall not give false testimony against your neighbor." Here we're reminded in very practical terms that social values learned in the family are lived out in the world. We don't just sit around taking a course in social values in the family, so that mom and dad can pat us on the head and say, "Well done, son, you've learned your social values." After we learn, they push us out of the nest and say, "Now go and live them out there where the action is."

You'll notice that these four commandments are all stated negatively. They could equally be stated positively, but God apparently assumed that we take more notice of things that are stated negatively. Suppose some kids on a summer's day discover a fence surrounding a factory. On it a notice says, "There is a factory within this fence and we're making all kinds of chemicals which are injurious to health. So we strongly advise you not to climb over this fence." It is highly improbable that they would take the warning very seriously. In fact, they would probably immediately devise ways of scaling the fence! However, if the same fence bore a sign with a great big skull and crossbones saying, "DANGER, KEEP OUT," it would more likely get their attention. That's what God is doing. He is putting up a skull and crossbones, saying DANGER, KEEP OUT—no murder, no adultery, no stealing, no false testimony. Keep away from these, because if you don't you'll find all kinds of things going wrong in your life. Let's look at these one at a time, stating each one positively.

- "You shall not murder" means, "Be totally committed to

the sanctity of human life." Most of us are familiar with the *King James Version* which says, "Thou shalt not kill." We need to understand that there are at least ten Hebrew words translated "kill" or its equivalent in the Old Testament. While the *King James Version* says, "Thou shalt not kill," it also teaches in the Book of Deuteronomy how to go to war, and when to exact capital punishment. The Bible would be self-contradictory if it said, "Thou shalt not kill" and then spoke approvingly of war and capital punishment. There is a place in Old Testament theology for war and for capital punishment, although it is not our purpose to develop these right now. The point is that when the Bible says, "You shall not kill," or as the *New International Version* has it, "You shall not murder," this is not a blanket prohibition on the taking of life, but a prohibition against taking life for reasons born of self-interest.

This is backed up by what Jesus said about people killing because of hatred: it is the hatred inside that is the root cause of the killing. What Jesus is suggesting is rather frightening. If I find my self-interest is such that I have a tremendous antipathy toward another person, and that antipathy can only adequately be described as hatred, then, given the right set of circumstances, I'm capable of killing! However, the probability of the right set of circumstances coming my way is remote; therefore, I need to be more concerned about my capacity for hatred than about the circumstances. If I have an attitude that in some way wants to get rid of or destroy another person, I have a mistaken perception of the intrinsic value of humanity. The biblical view is that man was created in the divine image for a divine purpose, and is capable of furthering the divine cause; for that reason Christians have the highest possible view of humanity, and regard human life as sacred. If they fail to maintain this regard, they are denying divine authority. If out of self-interest they destroy that which God has created, they are setting themselves above God; clearly, no covenant person can take that position.

But many people in our society do not view humanity from God's perspective. Secular people come in two varieties — pessimists and optimists. The pessimists say things like, "Man is what he eats. Man is a useless passion. Man is a being unto death. Man is a naked ape. Man is but a pipe, and his life but smoke. Man is the only animal that blushes or needs to. Man is an intelligence in servitude to his organs." With such a view of humanity, it's easy to see why these people don't care about human beings. They do not believe that mankind is created in the divine image, and they regard people as less than significant. As a result they debase the principle, "Do unto others as you wish they would do unto you!" into, "Do unto others before they do it unto you!" Such attitudes craft a sad society!

Of course, optimists are entirely different. Many of them are now into the New Age thinking. They reason, "All is one, all is god, therefore, we are god. If we don't know ourselves as god, it's because of our ignorance, and the only way to banish ignorance is through enlightenment that comes by meditation. If we can meditate properly, we will receive inner enlightenment and we will behave as gods. The answer to society's problems is not in a transcendent authority; the answer to society's problems is in ourselves." Purely secular, purely humanistic, and totally optimistic!

C.S. Lewis had a lovely statement about this kind of thinking, which is really historic *pantheism*. He said, "Pantheism is a creed not so much false, as hopelessly behind the times. Once, before creation, it would have been true to say that everything was God, but then God created, He caused things to be other than Himself."[3]

We live surrounded by pessimistic or optimistic humanists. The former insist that we are rushing headlong to perdition, the latter that we are meditating our way to paradise. But as they seem to head in opposite directions, they hold to one common thesis — that man, whatever he is, is not created in the divine image and therefore does not have eternal worth and significance.

If it is true that mankind has eternal significance, then our attitude toward people must be a reflection of this fact. Accordingly we will never allow self-interest to diminish or destroy a person created in the image of God. If that is clear in our thinking, our social values are clearly set. If that is not clear, our social values can be all over the ballpark.

• "You shall not commit adultery" means, "Be committed to the exclusiveness of marriage." Now remember that when you are talking about adultery, you're talking about sexual activity between people who are not married to each other. Suffice it to say that God is the One who ordained marriage. In the very beginning of Scripture we read, "For this reason a man will leave his father and mother and be united to his wife and they will become one flesh." That is rather straightforward. God ordained marriage! Not only does God make a powerful statement concerning marriage all through the Old Testament, but He also makes a powerful statement concerning the covenant, and then He consistently brings these two ideas together. In effect God says, "If you want to picture the covenant relationship that I have made with you, My people, look at marriage. In the same way that the husband commits himself to the wife and the wife commits herself to the husband, and they demonstrate that commitment by faithfulness, I have committed Myself to you and you are committing yourself to Me." The covenant faithfulness between God and His people was to be modelled by marital faithfulness. Now if God wanted to show that His covenant people were unfaithful to Him, what word would He use? Adultery. For in God's book adultery is the epitome of unfaithfulness, and is utterly abhorrent to Him.

The adulterer is engaging in activity that is destructive, deceptive, and degenerative. Such a person demonstrates dominant self-interest. You see, self-interest is the human problem over and over again, self-love gone to seed. Love for neighbor starts with love for spouse, the closest neighbor, and there is no greater way to love spouse than to be faithful to an exclusive marital covenant.

• "You shall not steal" means "Respect other people." One would almost assume that because it says, "You shall not steal," it means respect for the other person's property. While it includes property, it goes much further. In actual fact, the word translated "steal" means not so much to take property as to take another person's liberty. It almost has the connotation of "kidnap" or "hijack." Now there is a very real sense in which we can deprive a person of their property, but we need to broaden the scope to a recognition that we can also deprive a person of liberty, of opportunity, and of dignity. This can happen everywhere — it happens in marriages all the time. It happens in the business community. We may pride ourselves on the fact that we don't steal or take another person's property, but fail to realize that rampant self-interest can take over to such an extent that we won't even think twice about depriving a person of opportunity. We simply call it competition. We don't even think twice about depriving a person of dignity — we simply say they asked for it. We don't even think twice about depriving them of things that are theirs by God-given fiat; our self-interest has taken over.

A few years ago as I was coming out of my home early in the morning, I saw that my car's rear window had been broken. The radio and the tape deck and my collection of tapes had been stolen. Now, the car was an old heap anyway; I didn't need that tape recorder and radio, and I really didn't need all those tapes. My life was going to go on without them, and they were insured, so it didn't matter. Yet, I was amazed at my reaction: I was so angry, I was so hurt, I was so violated that somebody had actually done that to me. I didn't know who had done it. I was not aware that I had done something to anger anyone. Why would they come and take my property?

Why would they sneak into my place while I was asleep and do that to me? I thought, "I'm being totally irrational about this." Then I realized that my property was an extension of my person. To rob me of my property was to make a statement concerning the insignificance of my person. Then I thought how easy it is to simply violate people, their dignity, their opportunity, their property, their personality, and never even worry about it. And I was reminded about a simple principle: when self-interest runs riot, I may violate all kinds of people, even those I profess to love most. I need to check my social values.

● "You shall not give false testimony against your neighbor" means, "Be committed to integrity." If society is going to work, it has to have structures. There have to be things that people agree on. Some things need to be mandated with consequences of both reward and penalty, but we can't mandate everything. We have to have good will, cooperation, and trust. We can't function without trust. But if we're going to have trust, we need to live with integrity, and herein lies one of our problems. You see, we all have an inbuilt capacity to cheat. We cheat out of self-interest — how can we beat the system? How can we do the end run? How can we get ahead of the pack? It's in us, folks, it's in us! That's where a lack of integrity begins to show.

Let me illustrate how confused we are about integrity. The *Washington Post* and ABC News took a poll in April 1987 and discovered that two out of three Americans believed that Ronald Reagan was not telling the truth about the Iran scam. But the same poll said that by a margin of two to one, Americans believed that Ronald Reagan was an honest man! Two out of three believed he was lying, but by a margin of two to one they believed that he was an honest man. Presumably Americans in 1987 believed in honest liars! Now how do you figure that one out? Only by realizing that public concepts of integrity are very amorphous indeed. The French novelist Camus once said, "We stand in need of folk who have determined to speak directly and unmistakably and, come what may, to stand by what they have said." When you have integrity, respect, and faithfulness, and when you have a high view of man who is created in the divine image, you've got the raw materials for solid, social values. Where do you get them from? A transcendent authority who says, "Thus says the Lord."

You Shall Not Covet

The tenth commandment is distinct from the others in that it deals with attitudes rather than actions. It reminds us that societal values are lodged in the heart. They are learned in the family, they are lived out in the world, but they are lodged in the heart.

The problem in our society is self-interest run amuck. Another word for self-interest is "covetousness" or "inordinate desire." Now notice verse 21: "You shall not covet your neighbor's wife, you shall not set your desire on your neighbor's house." Two different Hebrew words, translated here as "covet" and "set desire on," both have to do with self-interest out of control—an attitude that makes me Number One and everything else secondary. This is a desire so dominant within me that anything goes; all that really matters is that I am what I am, and I do what I do, and I have what I have, and I'm doing things my way. Covetousness and inordinate desire lead to societal destruction in marriage, family, business, church—anywhere you get people rubbing shoulders.

The great privilege of the covenant people of God is that they get their values from a transcendent authority. They also recognize that in and of themselves they have not lived according to these instructions. That failure is called sin and they freely admit it and deeply repent of it. They come to Christ for forgiveness for it and they also draw on the resources of the indwelling Christ in the person of the Holy Spirit who enables them to live in newness of life.

The key to enjoying the good life is a right relationship with the living God. Right spiritual values translate into right human relationships by His standards of rightness, and produce righteous social values.

These are the commands, decrees and laws the Lord your God directed me to teach you to observe in the land that you are crossing the Jordan to possess, so that you, your children, and their children after them may fear the Lord your God as long as you live by keeping all His decrees and commands that I give you, and so that you may enjoy long life. Hear, O Israel, and be careful to obey so that it may go well with you and that you may increase greatly in a land flowing with milk and honey, just as the Lord, the God of your fathers, promised you.

"Hear, O Israel: The Lord our God, the Lord is one. Love the Lord your God with all your heart and with all your soul and with all your strength. These commandments that I give you today are to be upon your hearts. Impress them on your children. Talk about them when you sit at home and when you walk along the road, when you lie down and when get up. Tie them as symbols on your hands and bind them on your foreheads. Write them on the doorframes of your houses and on your gates.

"When the Lord your God brings you into the land He swore to your fathers, to Abraham, Isaac and Jacob, to give you—a land with large, flourishing cities you did not build, houses filled with all kinds of good things you did not provide, wells you did not dig, and vineyards and olive groves you did not plant—then when you eat and are satisfied, be careful that you do not forget the Lord, who brought you out of Egypt, out of the land of slavery.

"Fear the Lord your God, serve Him only and take your oaths in His name. Do not follow other gods, the gods of the peoples around you; for the Lord your God, who is among you, is a jealous God and His anger will burn against you, and He will destroy you from the face of the land. Do not test the Lord your God as you did at Massah. Be sure to keep the commands of the Lord your God and the stipulations and decrees He has given you. Do what is right and good in the Lord's sight, so that it may go well with you and you may go in and take over the good land that the Lord promised on oath to your forefathers, thrusting out all your enemies before you, as the Lord said."

Deuteronomy 6:1-19

FAMILY VALUES
OF THE GOOD LIFE

7 God created individuals; God invented society; and God ordained that families should be the basic structure of society. We need to reiterate this, because many social institutions today would try to give us the impression that the family is a human idea and that any notions people have about adjusting or changing the family are, therefore, perfectly legitimate. We have to recognize that the family is something which God ordained from the beginning of creation. It's rather interesting to notice that half of the Ten Commandments speak directly or indirectly about the family. When you realize that the Ten Commandments give us principles of operation right across the board, it does seem to me there is a disproportionate emphasis on the family.

I was reading an article recently entitled, "The American Family in the year 2000" that included this quote from the June 1983 *Futurist Magazine:* "It will not be uncommon for children born in the 1980s to live with both parents, then to live with their mothers after a divorce, and then live with their mothers and step-fathers, and then live alone for a time, and then live with someone of the opposite sex before marrying them, and then to marry, and then to divorce, and then to live alone, and then to remarry, and then to end up alone following the death of a spouse." That ought to give us pause. Many sociologists believe in a Darwinian approach to life, the basic principle of which is that everything is evolving for the better. Therefore, when they see the changes in the family, they automatically assume that this is simply an evolutionary change that will work for the good. One of those persons is Dr. Suzanne Keller, author of "Does the Family Have a Future?"

Perhaps someday we will cease to relate to families just as we no longer relate ourselves to clans. We may even see a world of uni-sex, multi-sex or non-sex. None of this can happen, however, if we refuse to shed some of our most cherished preconceptions such as that monogamy is superior to other forms of marriage or that women naturally make the best mothers. Much as we are convinced of these now, time may reveal them as yet another illusion.[4]

We Christians need to be concerning ourselves as to what the family is all about. There are three basic family values that I want to identify for you in this passage. First, *strong convictions* are absolutely necessary. Second, *genuine concerns* are absolutely crucial; and third, *clear communications* are absolutely vital. It was rather interesting to me after I had exegeted this passage to read an article by Dr. Nick Stinnett, chairman of the Department of Human Resources and Family Development at the University of Nebraska. He did a scholarly study of 3,000 families, all of whom rated themselves very high in marriage and family satisfaction. And he identified six characteristics of these strong families.

1. Strong families are made up of people who are committed to the concept of family.

2. Strong families are made up of people who spend time together.
3. Strong families always include good communication.
4. Strong families are made up of people who express appreciation.
5. Strong families have some kind of spiritual commitment.
6. Strong families have learned how to solve problems in crisis.

It's rather interesting to me that his findings have a marked degree of agreement with Scripture. This is very encouraging! It shows there are some sociologists on track!

Strong Convictions
"These commandments that I give you today are to be upon your hearts" (v. 6). We need deep and heartfelt convictions today as to what the family is all about. It is very easy for us to take our families for granted, to simply go with the flow as far as family life is concerned. But the flow may be heading for a spiritual and social Niagara.

I remember the first time Jill and I went out for an evening together. We went, of course, to a church service. We seem to have spent all our life in one ever since. After the service, we started talking to each other about our hopes and aspirations and I said to Jill, "You know, some time ago, Jill, God impressed deeply upon my heart that if I was ever going to marry, if I was ever going to have a family, it would be on this basis: 'As for me and my house we will serve the Lord.' " She started laughing, and said, "That is interesting because that is exactly the same thing God has impressed on my heart." So I said, "Why don't we get married then?" So we did and we've lived happily ever after! It didn't work quite that quickly, but close! Anyone contemplating marriage should make absolutely certain *before* they take the plunge that they know exactly what basis their family and marriage is going to have, and then that they find somebody in total agreement with this. If they don't, the chances of success are somewhat slim. Now what should these convictions relate to?

● First of all, there should be convictions about the *covenant.* You'll remember that the Book of Deuteronomy talks repeatedly about the idea of the covenant, and not only Deuteronomy, but the whole of the Bible. In fact, as we have pointed out, the word translated "testament" could be equally translated "covenant," so that we could say our Bible has an Old Covenant and New Covenant. Now if you aren't sure what covenant means, let me point out four powerful things that come through in Deuteronomy 5 and 6.

1. "The Lord our God, the Lord is one" (6:4). The existence and unity of God is something we should impress upon our children, something we are to communicate clearly to those for whom we have responsibility. In other words, Principle One is that the basis of our existence is the Lord Himself and we build our lives on Him.

2. According to Deuteronomy 5:6, this Lord is the One who reached out when He saw the people of Israel in distress and brought them out of their captivity. He didn't have to, but He took the initiative and in grace did for them what they couldn't do for themselves. Principle Two is that this God who exists sees the needs of His people, graciously takes the initiative, and intervenes in their affairs for their good.

3. We read in Deuteronomy 5:2 that this Lord who intervened in salvation and redemption for them made a covenant with His people. Principle Three is that God has committed Himself to a personal intimate relationship with His people.

4. The people were expected to respond by loving the Lord their God with all their heart and all their soul and all their strength, and to demonstrate it practically by loving their neighbors as themselves. That is Principle Four. And there you have the bones of the covenant.

Now I submit to you that if we are going to establish the families that God wants us to establish, we must do it with a strong conviction concerning the covenant. We need to build our families on a consciousness of who the Lord is, with immense gratitude for the fact that He has taken the initiative and intervened in our lives through redemption in Christ, and with thanks that He has made a covenant with us. Then our response will be obedience and reverence and love for Him and for those whom He has created.

Now it would be a good idea to sit down and ask yourself, "What are the fundamentals upon which our family is being built? Why does this family exist? What in the world are we trying to do in this family? Does our family have a motto?" If you don't have one, let me suggest the one that we've been operating on for over thirty years — "As for me and my house, we will serve the Lord." It was impossible for a child to be introduced into our family without their getting the message very quickly. Each one of them had to decide for themselves whether or not they wanted to get on board.

• Second, there are convictions concerning *commandments*. You will notice that verse 6 says, "These commandments that I give you today are to be upon your hearts." In other words, the convictions that are to be deeply impressed upon their hearts have to do with commandments. The great God who has graciously intervened in our lives expects us to lovingly respect Him and to demonstrate that respect by obeying His commands. It is not a matter of a harsh God laying rules and regulations on us; rather, it is a matter of a loving God desperately longing to see responsive love in our hearts, the evidence of which is obedience. "If you love Me," said Jesus, "keep My commandments."

Strong convictions about commandments require discipline, because there is something about all of us that isn't particularly anxious to be obedient. Discipline has to be built in if we are going to know what it means to live the life of loving

91

obedience. Now how do we learn obedience and discipline? You'll remember that the Scriptures teach us that God disciplines His people in much the same way fathers discipline children. God disciplines His people to learn obedience; therefore, it is a reasonable expectation that parents will discipline their children so that they will recognize that they cannot just run wild, but that there are certain principles to which they can reasonably be expected to adhere.

A number of years ago when Lou Holtz was coaching football at the University of Arkansas, his team was going to play for the national title in the Orange Bowl on New Year's Day. On the eve of the game, he shocked the boosters at the University of Arkansas by sending home three of his star players. His explanation was very simple, "They broke the rules." Well, there was a tremendous furor about it, of course, but it faded very quickly when he won the title without his three star players.

Subsequently, he went to the University of Minnesota, stayed there two years, turned their program around, and then went on to Notre Dame. When Notre Dame, in first place, was going to play the second place University of Southern California in the Los Angeles Coliseum, on the eve of this biggest game of the season, what did Lou Holtz do? He sent home two of his star players. When he was asked why, he simply said, "They broke the rules." The next day, of course, everything was forgotten and forgiven because he won again. When he was asked why he does this sort of thing, he replied to this effect, "It is more important that we teach young people to discipline their lives than it is that we win football games." He's right, of course!

Now the same obtains in the family. This means if we are to establish strong families, we must establish strong family values. This means deep convictions about the covenant, deep convictions about the commandments, and the discipline necessary to carry this through.

● Third, there are deep convictions concerning *consequences.*
Repeatedly in the Book of Deuteronomy we are reminded
that there are two options open to God's people. One is to
live in obedience and the other is to live in disobedience.
Moses instructed parents to tell their children, "The Lord
commanded us to obey all these decrees and to fear the Lord
our God, so that we might always prosper and be kept alive, as
is the case today. And if we are careful to obey all this law
before the Lord our God, as He has commanded us, that will
be our righteousness" (6:24-25).

If we are to live the good life, it will be the result of loving
obedience to God. There is a direct correlation between doing
it God's way and enjoying the good life as God describes it.
Conversely, we have noticed that troublesome statement in
the Ten Commandments about the sins of the fathers being
visited on the children to the third and fourth generations.
That means that when we fail in our families to adhere to
divine principles, it isn't just *our* lives that are affected, but
the lives of succeeding generations.

So the principle that we deeply impress upon our families
is, "There are consequences to our actions." If we live in
obedience, then we can expect God's blessing.

That does not mean that the land of milk and honey was *all*
milk and *all* honey. In actual fact, when they got into the land
flowing with milk and honey, the first thing they confronted
was giants in the land. Then they discovered there were all
kinds of opposition. Life was a perpetual battle. They soon
learned the good life is not a life of ease—God did not promise them a rose garden.

The good life is one spent adhering to divine principles and
knowing the blessings of God. But conversely, all kinds of
ramifications and repercussions result if we do not live according to His principles. This may be a little hard for us to
swallow so let me quote Chuck Swindoll. "In today's terms,
our fathers sinned but we bought the farm. Our fathers ate

the meal and we picked up the tab. There is a lot of litter today thanks to yesterday's trash and the family is the place where all the garbage stacks up."[5]

Actions do have consequences and we should reckon on the results before we embark on the activity. If we are to build strong families, we need to establish strong convictions concerning the covenant, convictions concerning the commandments, and convictions about the consequences.

Genuine Concerns

We are not to think just in terms of a strong, austere disciplined family. Far from it. For in a family which is predicated on the love and grace of God and a loving response to God, while that love is demonstrated by disciplined obedience, there will also be a genuine concern for the people who are part of the family. This comes in three different forms.

● First there will be the genuine concern of the parent for the children. As we are moving more and more away from the idea of community to individualism, it is not uncommon now for parents to break up a family because they as individuals are not fulfilled; they seem to give little or no thought to the ramifications of this for the dependent children in that family. I am absolutely convinced that where there is a strong family, there will be a genuine concern for the well-being of the children. Parents will be willing to subjugate their own selfish concerns to the well-being of those children. Let me tell you why. The children did not ask to be brought into the world; their birth was the result of the activity of their parents.

One day a boy said to his father, "I did not ask to be born into this family." "No," said his father, "and if you had, the answer would have been no!"

Given that children are part of the family because of the initiative of the parents, it is perfectly obvious to me that the parents carry responsibility for the children. This comes through very clearly in the delightful expression, "You saw how the Lord your God carried you, as a father carries his son, all the way you went until you reached this place" (1:31). The idea of a caring, carrying concern on the part of the parents for the child is a fundamental value which has to be established in the family. But it isn't a one-way street.

● Second, there is the concern of children for parents. "Honor your father and mother so you may live long and it may go well with you" hardly needs repeating at this juncture. The reciprocal concern of the children for their parents to honor them, respect and, whenever possible, to express appreciation to them, is clearly expected. How dilatory we are in expressing appreciation to one another!

You heard about the little boy who was talking to the old man. The man asked, "What is your name?"

"Bobby."

"Is that your only name?"

"No, my full name is Bobby-don't-do-it."

It is possible for a little boy to grow up honestly thinking his name is, "Bobby-don't-do-it" because that's all he ever hears. And it is possible for parents to get the idea, once their children have taken Psyc. 101, that they are the biggest dummies in the world. A little appreciation, some genuine reciprocal concern, and an honoring of the parents for the things that they have done right is most appropriate.

Now some people are going to say, "Hey, if you knew my parents you wouldn't expect me to honor them." I think Jesus could help us with this one. He knew His parents pretty well and they weren't perfect either. They took Jesus to Jerusalem on the Feast Day. Hundreds of people trekked all the way down from Galilee to Jerusalem and had a wonderful celebration. Then it was time to head north again. So off the crowd went, and the parents of Jesus, for some inexplicable reason, assumed that He was with them. They thought, "He's a good Boy and He'll know exactly what to do; everybody else is coming along, so we'll assume He is all right."

At the end of the day, they got the shock of their lives—He wasn't there. They had failed in their responsibility to this rather important Child of theirs. They panicked, went rushing back to Jerusalem, and searched high and low. Eventually they looked in the temple and saw their adolescent Son having a theological debate with the professors of theology, asking them questions, giving them answers. When they saw Him, they were amazed. They didn't even understand their own Child. He knew they didn't understand Him, and so He asked, "Don't you understand I must be about My Father's business?" And His parents said, "Huh?"

What an interesting family we have here! Parents who blow it by assuming that the child is being cared for when He isn't, who panic when everything doesn't work out the way they expect it to, who don't understand their own child, and when He explains himself to them haven't a clue what He is talking about. Then notice how His mother reacts, "Why have You done this to us?" A reasonable response on His part would have been, "I thought you did it to Me!" But that's what parents are like—sometimes they blame the children, when the blame should attach to the parents. Granted, Joseph and Mary had a formidable task caring for their child. It's easy to see their failure.

The point of the story, however, is this: as inadequate as they clearly were, "Jesus went with them and was obedient to them." Honor your father and mother. However imperfect your parents are, make sure there is some way in which you respect them. Conversely, you parents, however difficult your children may be, make sure your behavior merits respect. Here is the concern coming through—the concern of the parents for the child, the concern of the child for the parents.

• But there is a third concern. Over and over again in the Book of Deuteronomy, instructions are given concerning widows, orphans, slaves, aliens, the underprivileged, the dispossessed of society. There is much talk today about the traditional family. We should remember that the traditional family as often portrayed today—mom who stays at home, dad who goes out and earns the bacon, 2.3 kids, a dog and a TV—is a relatively recent creation, exclusive to the affluent West. You are very hard put to find that kind of family in bygone generations in our culture, or in other parts of the world today. The traditional family in biblical times, and to this day in many parts of the world, consisted of mother and father both working in the field, lots and lots of kids, lots of uncles and aunts, grandparents, manservants, maidservants, slaves, aliens, widows and a whole bunch of orphans—a household. Far from being a contemporary traditional family which is self-contained and often self-absorbed, it was a family that had a tremendous concern, not only of parents for children and children for parents, but of both parents and children for others who needed a home.

I want to be sensitive when I speak about the family, because I know there are many people who have very unhappy family situations. There is no shortage of those who look askance at what their parents have done and feel they are suffering as a result. Many are the victims of divorce; others are the perpetrators of divorce; and still others are the children of divorce. It's almost like rubbing salt in the wounds when we talk about the family according to Scripture. We don't want to rub salt into anybody's wounds, but we must outline the principles that God has ordained, and these include caring for widows, orphans, etc. The solid, healthy families in the church have a responsibility and an obligation to be adopting into their families the modern day widows and orphans and the aliens. Who are they? They are those who are the products of the fractured, fragmented families. Many sit next to us in the pews, but far more sit alone in ill-lit apartments waiting to be cared for and encouraged.

When our children were growing up, there were always all kinds of folks in our home who were in need of help and encouragement. So our kids thought that that was how every family operated. Example is the best way in the world to give your children an understanding of what it really means to live out a balance of conviction and concern.

Clear Communications

"These commandments that I give you today are to be upon your hearts. Impress them on your children. Talk about them . . . " (6:6). "In the future when your son asks you . . . tell him" (6:20-21). What's all this about? It is about communication!

In his summary in Deuteronomy 32, Moses said, "These are not just idle words for you—they are your life" (v. 47). The well-known statement, "Man does not live on bread alone but on every word that comes from the mouth of the Lord God" is also found in Deuteronomy (8:3). When we're thinking in terms of building the family on the covenant, and teaching commandments and concern and consequences, what we're really saying is this: God has communicated to us and it is imperative that we be communicating with each other; otherwise, how are these principles going to be established? Who is going to do it, if we don't?

Communication, of course, goes two ways. It requires talking and listening. I love verse 20: "In the future when your son asks you . . . ," for it clearly assumes an environment where parents spend enough time with their kids for the children to ask them intelligent questions. Now that is not always the case. For some reason we bring these kids into the world, we decide that they should exist, we put them into our families—and then we let them get on with their lives while we get on with ours. Whenever and wherever these lives collide, we hope the collision will be minimized, instead of building a relationship in which there is clear communication between child and parent. We should be working toward an atmosphere where the child feels free to ask and the parent is willing and able to answer. Verse 22 does not say, "In the future when your son asks you what is the meaning of the stipulations, decrees, and laws the Lord our God has commanded, you tell him to go and ask his mother." It is not, "Go and ask the youth pastor; I'm busy." There is a simple, basic responsibility for the parents to be listening to what their children have to say, to be encouraging their inquiry, and to be developing skills to be able to talk intelligently to the children about what life is, predicated on the covenant. That's what we are supposed to be doing. Clear communication.

• Notice also that this communication is intended to be the most natural thing in the world. Now I know there are some people who don't start off very well with their kids — they park them in Sunday School, pick them up, and take them home. They can't be bothered to be involved spiritually in their adolescence. Then, when the kids start going off the rails, the parents suddenly try to impose some spiritual values, and they feel hurt because the kids are disinterested. The kids aren't stupid. They simply say, "We've managed all this time without spiritual values. Why are you suddenly laying them on us now?"

This problem has to do with there being a sense of artificiality about spiritual life. We need to make sure that in the most natural way imaginable we are teaching our children about all the ramifications of life based on the covenant. Why do I keep emphasizing "the natural way"? Verse 7 says, "Impress [these things] on your children. Talk about them when you sit at home, and when you walk along the road, when you lie down and when you get up." Four descriptions of the most natural life situations. Sitting around at home, walking along the road, going to bed, and having breakfast. That's family life isn't it? It's in the context of this most natural setting that all these principles about life are to be shared and communicated. The problem with sitting at home and talking with each other is that we don't always do it!

On my first trip to the U.S.A., I was in Southern California staying with friends. I got up in the morning and by 3:00 in the afternoon, we still hadn't had anything to eat. I finally did say to the hostess, "My stomach thinks my throat is cut."

She said, "Huh?"

"I said my stomach thinks my throat is cut."

"Oh," she said, "that's a joke."

Just then her son came in and said something that sounded like, "Dyeatyet?"

His mother replied, "Notyetdyou?"

I tried to understand what was going on. I was being introduced to a new approach to eating. Instead of the European mealtime, I was being introduced to the "grab a bite" mentality. What a lovely thing it is to be part of a family that sits down together and has time to talk and time to listen.

How great it is when a family has time to walk along the road together. Now I must admit that I didn't do a lot of walking with my kids when they were growing up, but I taught all three of them how to run. As we ran together, we talked. I do remember, however, on one occasion about twenty years ago, when I went for a walk with my son Dave. He was about ten years old and the British school system had decided to teach sex education. The teacher in the little school our kids went to called us and said, "This really is rather ironic — you are married and I am single, and I have the job of teaching your children about sex. So, I want all the parents to come and see what I'm going to teach your children, see the videos that the BBC is going to share with them, and tell me if they're all right." Our kids knew we were going to school — they knew it was about sex and they were agog. They were thrilled, they were excited, they couldn't wait to hear what happened. When we got back, we told them what had happened, that they were going to have some sex education and that the teacher wanted to share it with us, and that we told her it was fine. Weeks later it occurred to me that we never heard a word about it. So I took Dave and my golden retriever for a walk along a country lane, late at night. I thought this was a good time to talk about sex with my boy, in the dark.

"Dave, did you have that sex education in school?"

"Yep."

"Do you want to talk about it?"

"Nope."

"Don't you think we should talk about it?

"Nope."

"Well, have you no comments to make about it?"

"Yeah, what's all the fuss about?"

"What fuss?"

"Well, everybody seems to be fussing about this thing. Teachers are worried about it, all the parents are worried about it, and all the kids are worried about it. What's the fuss about?" And I thought, "Praise God! No fuss as far as he's concerned." We'd talked with him along the way and told him about it — the most natural thing in the world.

And when you lie down at night, you communicate with your children as well. That doesn't just mean you tuck the little rascals into bed and get them to pray. It also means that when your children are teenagers and they come in late from a date, and you are already in bed — father's asleep and mother's awake because there is no point in both of them staying awake — and your daughter comes in and says she has just had the most wonderful date and then she tells you about it, you say, "Praise God, who cares about sleep — she wants to talk about her date. She wants to share with us what's happening in her life!" I remember my daughter coming in from a date on one occasion, so excited that she said, "I can't sleep, Dad. Let's go for a run." I said, "Judy, I'm in bed, I've already been asleep, it's past midnight." She said, "You're no fun at all." To prove what fun I was, I got up and ran with her, praising God that she wanted to be with me, to talk and share.

These family values are not only to be established, but they are to be expressed. "Tie them as symbols on your hands, bind them on your foreheads, write them on the door frames of your houses and on your gates." Because Orthodox Jewish people take this literally, they wear a philactery when they pray, a little box on the forehead between their eyes in which is a parchment on which is written selections of Scripture, many of them from Deuteronomy. On the doorpost of their house, they nail a mazuzzah containing a portion of Scripture. While we take these words more metaphorically, there is something very significant here. If you have these principles between your eyes (that's the literal expression here), they control your mind-set. And if you have them bound on your hands, they are applied in your daily business. If they are displayed on the doorposts of your home, the family operates on divine principles. And if they are nailed to your gate—that's the gate of your public life, your commitments are clearly recognized.

These family values should also be emulated. Notice that Deuteronomy talks not only about your children's children unto the third and fourth generation, but also about "your fathers" and "your forefathers"—Abraham, Isaac, Jacob, you, your children, your grandchildren, third generation, fourth generation. . . . The point is that this covenant is supposed to be continued. This covenant relationship will be continued to the extent that individual families keep the chain intact. If there is one thing your family should be concerned about, it is establishing the covenant so firmly that succeeding generations catch the momentum and maintain the covenant relationship.

For those of you who don't have a heritage of this kind, let me encourage you—start one! Build your family on this principle: "As for me and my house, we will serve the Lord."

Be careful to follow every command I am giving you today, so that you may live and increase and may enter and possess the land that the Lord promised on oath to your forefathers. Remember how the Lord your God led you all the way in the desert these forty years, to humble you and to test you in order to know what was in your heart, whether or not you would keep His commands. He humbled you, causing you to hunger and then feeding you with manna, which neither you nor your fathers had known, to teach you that man does not live on bread alone but on every word that comes from the mouth of the Lord. Your clothes did not wear out and your feet did not swell during these forty years. Know then in your heart that as a man disciplines his son, so the Lord your God disciplines you.

"When you have eaten and are satisfied, praise the Lord your God for the good land He has given you. Be careful that you do not forget the Lord your God, failing to observe His commands, His laws and His decrees that I am giving you this day. Otherwise, when you eat and are satisfied, when you build fine houses and settle down, and when your herds and flocks grow large and your silver and gold increase and all you have is multiplied, then your heart will become proud and you will forget the Lord your God, who brought you out of Egypt, out of the land of slavery. He led you through the vast and dreadful desert, that thirsty and waterless land, with its venomous snakes and scorpions. He brought you water out of hard rock. He gave you manna to eat in the desert, something your fathers had never known, to humble and to test you so that in the end it might go well with you. You may say to yourself, 'My power and the strength of my hands have produced this wealth for me.' But remember the Lord your God, for it is He who gives you the ability to produce wealth, and so confirms His covenant, which He swore to your forefathers, as it is today.

"If you ever forget the Lord your God and follow other gods and worship and bow down to them, I testify against you today that you will surely be destroyed. Like the nations the Lord destroyed before you, so you will be destroyed for not obeying the Lord your God."

Deuteronomy 8:1-5, 10-20

THE GOOD LIFE
AND ITS PERILS

8 As Moses continued to brief the Children of Israel concerning the new land where they were going to live, he emphasized the perils attached to the good life.

A number of years ago the Soviet Union moved forces into Afghanistan, and as the Soviet forces moved in, tens of thousands of Afghans moved out and went into political exile in neighboring Pakistan. When President Gorbachev announced that the forces of the Soviet Union would withdraw and return to their homeland, the refugees moved out of Pakistan and began to return to their homeland. What they didn't know, however, was that there were between 5 and 15 million land mines buried beneath the surface separating the returning refugees from their villages. Many of the people went rushing back to their villages only to be blown to pieces. Some lost limbs; many lost their lives. There were perils in the good land. The tragedy was that they were not warned.

As the people of God prepared to move into the Promised Land, they were warned that while the good life in the good land was full of good things, it was also fraught with perils. They needed to be forewarned in order that they might be forearmed, and the same principle applies for the people of God in all generations.

Possibilities

In order that we might see the context correctly, let me remind you of some of the possibilities of the good life that God outlines for His people. He pointed out to them, "You are a people holy to the Lord your God. The Lord your God has chosen you out of all the peoples on the face of the earth to be His people, His treasured possession" (7:6).

● There was a very real sense in which they were going into the Promised Land enjoying individual, personal blessing. But they were to clearly understand that they were not just to enjoy these things individually, but were to go in as a *corporate unity*. They were to be clearly recognizable as the *people* of God.

This was important because the nations that surrounded the land in which the people of Israel were going to live were full of all kinds of problems. Like societies ever since the Fall, they were fragmenting and fracturing. God was concerned to put a corporate people in the midst of them to show the fragmenting and fracturing nations what society can be when it operates under the divine dictates. They were to be a holy people and that meant they were to be distinct, to be different, to stand out in the crowd.

Their distinction was to come directly from the fact that they were prepared to be the people of God. They were not to operate according to the cultural mores of the societies around about them, but were to be uniquely and distinctively different and holy. They were to understand that God had invested a lot in them and they were His treasured possession. He was counting on them to be His people. He could have chosen any of the peoples—it was not that Israel was particularly strong or righteous or holy. In fact, God went out of His way to tell them that they were none of these things. The only reason they were His people was that He had sovereignly chosen that they should be. He had chosen to set His love upon them. They were privileged people, but they were accordingly responsible.

The people of God are His people not because they are particularly righteous, not because they are particularly moral, not because they are particularly special. They are the people of God because He has sovereignly chosen to take the initiative of moving into their lives and drawing them to Himself, individually, in order that they might live collectively as an alternate society. The church of Jesus Christ is intended to be a corporate group operating under divine dictates, holy, separate, distinct, different, living individually and collectively in a challenging positive way in the midst of a fracturing and fragmenting society. This then is our privilege — to be a treasured possession. That was one of the possibilities confronting the people as they moved into the Promised Land.

● But notice another possibility about which Moses took great pains to warn them. He told them that they were going to find at least seven nations occupying the territory that God had given to them, and they were to move those people out. They were, in actual fact, to obliterate these people. They were to obliterate all signs of their culture and to destroy all evidence of their religion. This poses problems for us as it no doubt did for them. We do, however, need to recognize that God was dealing with the inhabitants of the land in this way because of the awesomeness and awfulness of their sin. The people of Israel in removing them and their cultures were functioning as instruments of divine judgment. But that was only part of the story. God insisted that the people of Israel should move these people out and obliterate their culture and their religion because if they didn't, there was the possibility that the people of Israel, far from being holy and distinct and different, would become ensnared with the alien culture. Far from being an example to the nations, they would become ensnared by cultures that were in diametric opposition to all that God stood for. Instead of being an example of righteousness, they would become indistinguishable from the cultures that were antithetical to God. This has always been the danger for the people of God.

Today we have different ways of dealing with this. Many of us recognize that as members of the covenant people of God, we live in an alien culture. So our way of coping is to separate ourselves and build up barriers so that we will not become infected. We are strong on being holy, we're strong on being separate, we're strong on being distinct. The problem with that approach, however, is that while we are avoiding being ensnared by an alien culture, we're doing absolutely nothing in terms of ministry to it. On the other hand, if we begin to identify with an alien culture in order that we might minister, then it is very easy for us to be sucked into it and become ensnared. Jesus summarized this magnificently when He talked about being "in the world but not of it." We are in it to be an example; we are not of it, because then we'd be ensnared. And therein lies the fundamental tension for the people of God in an alien culture.

Now as we see these two possibilities that confronted the people of God as they moved into the Promised Land, we need to be aware of them for ourselves, individually and collectively—the possibility of being an example to a fragmenting society, and the possibility of being ensnared by an alien culture. How do we stand firm and tall so that our distinctives are clear for all to see? How do we ensure that our distinctives are not a total "turn off" to other people? How do we retain an attraction about us that gives us an "in" into the thinking and consciousness of the society we want to impact?

Perils
The perils of the good life, they were told, would come in two particular forms. There would be the *obvious perils* from the

opposition—from the Hittites, the Girgashites, Amorites, Canaanites, Perizzites, Hivites and Jebusites (7:1). We don't know if this is an exhaustive list; there are some scholars who believe that there were also Termites. What we do know, however, is that all these "ites" were not going to roll over and play dead. They were going to defend their territory and fight for their land. They were going to resist the invaders tooth and nail.

God had made it very clear to the Israelites that they were outnumbered; in themselves, they didn't have what it would take to overthrow the people who were inhabiting the land. He had made them a promise that He would give them the land and would fight for them, but they had to go in and possess it. There is a fine balance here again. God didn't say, "I'm going to give you the land; put your feet up and take it easy by the Red Sea." He didn't say either, "If you want the land you'd better go in there and get it. You're on your own now." It wasn't all up to God and it wasn't all up to them. It was all up to them *because* it was all up to God.

We find the same balance in the New Testament. Christians are told, "Be strong in the Lord and in the power of His might!" There is obvious opposition to the Christian cause all over the world. The commission of the Church of Jesus Christ is to move into areas of opposition, strong in the Lord and in the power of His might, and to stand tall and to stay true. It's going to take all the resources of God to enable the church to do it and it's going to take all the dedication of the church to utilize His resources. If we don't do this, we may be overwhelmed by the obvious opposition that confronts us individually and collectively.

It is interesting to note that God said, "The Lord your God will drive out those nations before you little by little" (7:22). He was not just going to zap the nations, kick them all out, obliterate them all with a massive earthquake, and then say to the people of Israel who had been lolling around on the shore of Jordan, "There it is on a silver platter, enjoy!" He said, "You're going to go in there to fight the battles in My power, and you're only going to win little by little." The reason? "You will not be allowed to eliminate them all at once or the wild animals will multiply around you." If God had simply eradicated all the people, as He was perfectly capable of doing, and then had handed the Promised Land to the people of Israel, they would not have been strong enough or numerous enough to inhabit all the land, and so it would have been overrun by wild animals. So God, very wisely if I may say so, promised they would overcome "little by little."

So it is in the Christian life. There is no such thing as a victorious experience that hands victory to you on a plate for the rest of your life. You enjoy triumph and victory in your spiritual experience as you fight in all the power of God who fights for you situation by situation, and you win little by little. If that were not the case, then you would simply relax and the wild animals would overpower you and you would be back to square one. There are perils on every hand.

There would also be the *subtle perils* that came from the *self.* It's often easy for us to recognize the external opponents of our individual spiritual life and of the collective life of the church. It is much more difficult for us to identify the perils that are internal, that are found innately in the human breast, that are discovered in the inner life of those who constitute the body of Christ. The subtle perils come from the self. Dr. Paul Vitz, Professor of Psychology at New York University in his book *Psychology as Religion: The Cult of Self-Worship* wrote,

It should be obvious . . . that the relentless and singleminded search for and glorification of the self is at direct cross purposes with the Christian injunction to *lose* the self. Certainly Jesus Christ neither lived nor advocated a life that would qualify by today's standards as "self-actualized." For the Christian the self is the problem, not the potential paradise. Understanding this problem involves an awareness of sin, especially of the sin of pride; correcting this condition requires the practice of such un-self-actualized states as contrition and penitence, humility, obedience and trust in God.[6]

There is a preponderance in our society of what Dr. Vitz terms "selfism" psychology. And the basic tenet of this "selfism" psychology is that there is a potential paradise within us in the self. And if we can simply actualize the self, then we will discover paradise. Christianity must take strong opposition to this concept, for the self is the problem, not the paradise. Let's look at ways in which God warned the people of Israel against the subtle perils of the self.

• There are the perils of *self-interest*. Now we all recognize that the basic tenet of our society is that people are going to do most things out of self-interest. But self-interest run to seed produces all kinds of fragmentation in the society. And so some people say that what we need is enlightened self-interest. God, however, pointed out to the Israelites that if they operated on the basis of self-interest, whether enlightened or unenlightened, it would only be a matter of time until self-interest overcame interest in the things of God. If they made alliances with the people of the land out of self-interest, it might make a lot of sense in the short term, but in the long run, it could be disastrous.

Look at it this way. If they had to go into the land as a member of the people of Israel and obey God and exterminate the people there, it would be messy and it would not make a lot of practical sense. They probably wouldn't want to do it. On the other hand, they could look at the people and say, "They sure know how to farm this land and I don't know one end of a hoe from the other; maybe we should get them to help us. Then maybe we should have a political and military alliance and to solidify this we should marry our sons to their daughters and their daughters to our sons. This will clearly be in our best interest."

But God said, "If you do that, you will make a covenant, (that's the word He uses here) with those people who are the opponents of the One with whom you have made the primary covenant, the living God." It is the easiest thing in the world for the people of God to make alliances and covenants with those who are in fundamental opposition to the covenant God. And when they do this out of self-interest, the things of God begin to take a backseat. We've seen it over and over again.

I remember a young lady coming to talk to me on one occasion. She had become engaged to a young man in college and she wanted me to perform the marriage ceremony. I asked her about him and she told me all about him. Then I asked about his spiritual life and she said, "Well, he's not a believer, but I know he'll become one once we are married." And so I said, "I understand. Would you do something for me?' I got a chair and put it in the middle of the room and then I said, "I need to ask you please to stand on this chair." She looked a little nervous about it and I said, "It's a perfectly nice chair; please stand on it." So she stood on the chair and I said, "You are now standing on a higher plane than I am, and I want you to look at me as if I am your fiancé — it will take a tremendous stretch of your imagination, but try. Now, please hold my hands and lift me onto your higher plane." Do you know what happened? She fell off the chair. Surprise, surprise! It should come as no surprise that people who stand on chairs and try to lift people from the floor to the chair are likely to fall off and land on the floor. The analogy is obvious. If covenant people make covenants with those they are trying to lift to higher levels, what usually happens is that they don't lift anyone, but they come toppling down themselves.

• Then there is the peril of *self-indulgence.* In the wilderness, Moses said, "He humbled you, causing you to hunger and then feeding you with manna, which neither you nor your fathers had known, to teach you that man does not live on bread alone but on every word that comes from the mouth of the Lord" (8:3). While they were in the wilderness, they were utterly dependent on God, and He gave them manna every morning. Now manna is a Hebrew word which translates into English as "What is it?" For forty years, they had "What is it?" for every meal. They detested it—that's obvious because for forty years they never gave it a name. Every day, three times a day, they had "What is it?" The important thing is that it kept them alive. But now they were coming into the Promised Land where bread would not be scarce. Whole wheat, crushed wheat, pumpernickel, raisin bread, you name it, it would be there. Imagine the delights of delicious fresh baked bread after that wretched "What is it?" for forty years!

Therein lies the peril of self-indulgence. They could become so excited about the variety and abundance of the new life that they would simply indulge in all these things and forget something. The only reason they survived for forty years in the wilderness was that God's Word was operative in their lives. When they obeyed it, God worked; and when they didn't, He didn't work. But once they would have the abundance of bread, who would need God's Word? They would have all they needed and could simply fill themselves full and ignore the divine principle. They could indulge themselves in the material at the expense of the spiritual.

If I were to ask you if you believe that man does not live by bread alone, but by every word that proceeds out of the mouth of God, you would say, "I do believe it." Let me ask you something, "How is your spiritual health and what exactly is your spiritual caloric intake on a daily basis?" It's one thing to nod our heads wisely and say man does not live by indulging in material things only, but by indulging in the things that come from God. But it's another thing to battle the indulgence in material things that so readily supercedes a hunger for spiritual reality. We nod our heads wisely and then wonder why we are physically and materially indulgent and spiritually emaciated. You know why it is? Because we will indulge ourselves materially at the expense of our spiritual well-being, and therein lies another peril of the good life — the peril of self-indulgence.

● Then there is the peril of *self-sufficiency*. Notice this very poignant passage from Deuteronomy 8:12.

When you eat and are satisfied, when you build fine houses and settle down, and when your herds and flocks grow large and your silver and gold increase and all you have is multiplied, then your heart will become proud and you will forget the Lord your God, who brought you out of Egypt, out of the land of slavery. He led you through the vast and dreadful desert, that thirsty and waterless land, with its venomous snakes and scorpions. He brought you water out of hard rock. He gave you manna to eat in the desert, something your fathers had never known, to humble and to test you so that in the end it might go well with you. You may say to yourself, "My power and the strength of my hands have produced this wealth for me." But remember the Lord your God, for it is he He who gives you the ability to produce wealth.

I discovered these verses when I was a teenager, and I remember underlining them heavily; they have been a fundamental principle in my life ever since. It is God who gives us the ability to get wealth. The epitome of self-sufficiency is for us to acquire a beautiful home, and cars and all the wonderful material things that God has blessed us with (He gives us all things richly to enjoy) and to heap them to ourselves and say, *"We did it."* And God says, "How dare you! You never created a single thing! All that you have, you have because I, the Creator, graciously allowed you to enjoy it."

Oh, the audacity of self-sufficiency. Prosperity can very easily lead to pride. The Lord Jesus underlined the principle in the New Testament. A certain man had a great year on his farm and finished up with a bumper crop. An excellent businessman, good-looking, energetic, innovative, he said, "I know what I'll do—I'll pull down my barns and start all over again. I'll store everything up and take an early retirement. I've worked hard and I deserve it. I'll go to Florida and play golf. And I'll say to myself, 'Take your ease, eat, drink and be merry. You absolutely deserve all you've got.' " And God leaned out of heaven and characterized this man's endeavors with one scathing word, "FOOL! Tonight your soul will be required of you. Then whose will these things be?" How much did that man leave? Everything! And whose were the things that he thought were his? The One they truly belonged to—the eternal God.

Self-sufficiency means that I convince myself that all the answers are in me and I don't need God. The remarkable irony of this is that self-sufficiency afflicts those who have received most bountifully at the hands of the God they now ignore. Prosperity leads to pride and pride leads to a sense of power and power blinds me to the One who provides.

It's rather interesting to notice that when the dreadful earthquake hit Soviet Armenia that the Soviet Union publicly asked for and received help. What's interesting about this is that they had never done it before. They couldn't do it before because you see Marxist ideology states that the Marxist state is self-sufficient; therefore, to admit a need and to ask for help would be a fundamental denial of their ideology. So how did they handle it before Glasnost? When they had a tragedy and a need, they put a blackout of news on it; they denied there was a problem and they simply let the people suffer, because to have admitted a need and to ask for help would have struck at the very root of their ideology. Isn't it wonderful that the self-sufficient Marxists are admitting there are times when they are not self-sufficient? Now we need to pray that capitalists will discover the same thing. Instead of believing that what we have, we earned, and what we have, we made, and that we can go it alone, sooner or later, preferably sooner, we will admit it is He who gives us the ability to get wealth and acknowledge our total dependency upon Him.

● There are the perils of *self-righteousness.* "After the Lord your God has driven them [that is the seven nations] out before you, do not say to yourself, 'The Lord has brought me here to take possession of this land because of my righteousness' " (9:4). The self-righteousness that was latent within the breast of these Israelites is in all of us. We think, but dare not say, "See where I live, see the blessings I've got—do you know why I live here and do you know why I've got what I've got? Because I deserve it, that's why I have what I've got. I worked hard for it and God saw me work hard, and He said, 'You're a good man and you are not like those others, so I'll bless you.' I deserve it all." That is the essence of self-righteousness. God sticks a pin in that bubble very quickly. To the Israelites He said, "It's not because of your righteousness or your integrity that you are going in to take possession of their land. . . . Understand, then, that it is not because of your righteousness that the Lord your God is giving you this good land to possess, for you are a stiff-necked people" (9:5-6). Anybody who thinks that he can earn salvation and deserve blessing is at heart self-righteous and understands little of the grace of God.

There is another kind of self-righteousness that comes up in our society and it's related to the "selfism" psychology. The idea is that somehow we deserve all the blessings, but we don't deserve any of the problems. Our problems have nothing to do with us—they are somebody else's fault. I came across a beautiful summary of this in a "psychiatric folk song" (whatever that is), by Anna Russell that expresses the prevailing self-righteousness of our society.

116

At three I had a feeling of ambivalence
   towards my brothers,
and so it followed naturally,
   I poisoned all my lovers,
but now I'm happy. I have learned
   the lessons this has taught —
that everything I do that's wrong
   is someone else's fault.[7]

● Then there is the peril of *self-assertiveness*. I fully recognize that self-assertiveness is necessary at times; but when it degenerates into a rebellious spirit and a resistant attitude toward God, we're in deep peril. God told His people, "You are a stiff-necked people. Remember this and never forget how you provoked the Lord your God to anger" (9:6-7).

One of my favorite preachers when I was growing up was Campbell McAlpine. We loved him so much we called our eldest boy after him, David Stanley Campbell Briscoe. I remember Campbell was preaching one day. He looked at us all and said, "God told His ancient people that they were a stiff-necked people. How many stiff-necked people are here tonight? Let me explain what else God said. He said to His ancient people, 'You have turned your backs to Me but not your faces.' Try it. And that's how you get a stiff neck."

But what does it mean to turn your back on God but not your face? To turn your face to God all the time is to say all the right words and to put on the right smile, to have everything right in theory; to turn your back to Him at the same time means that while you're pretending everything is right, in reality you're going your own way. This is the essence of a self-assertive spirit that is rebellious and resistant.

Now look again at the perils to the good life, the obvious perils from the opposition, the subtle perils from the self. What precautions do we need to take to be able to move into a land-mine-infested good land?

Remember the past,
Remember where we were,
Remember what God did,
Remember who He is.
Remember the principles.

Principle 1. You are a holy people.
Principle 2. You are totally dependent on divine grace.
Principle 3. You do not live by bread alone.
Principle 4. You didn't make it this far on your own.

Remember the perils. There are land mines whichever way you go.

Remember the praise. "When you have eaten and are satisfied, praise the Lord your God for the good land *He* has *given* you." Remember the praise (8:10).

Observe the month of Abib and celebrate the Passover of the Lord your God, because in the month of Abib He brought you out of Egypt by night. Sacrifice as the Passover to the Lord your God an animal from your flock or herd at the place the Lord will choose as a dwelling for His name. Do not eat it with bread made with yeast, but for seven days eat unleavened bread, the bread of affliction, because you left Egypt in haste—so that all the days of your life you may remember the time of your departure from Egypt. Let no yeast be found in your possession in all your land for seven days. Do not let any of the meat you sacrifice on the evening of the first day remain until morning. . . .

"Count off seven weeks from the time you begin to put the sickle to the standing grain. Then celebrate the Feast of Weeks to the Lord your God by giving a freewill offering in proportion to the blessings the Lord your God has given you. And rejoice before the Lord your God at the place He will choose as a dwelling for His Name. . . .

"Celebrate the Feast of Tabernacles for seven days after you have gathered the produce of your threshing floor and your winepress. Be joyful at your Feast—you, your sons and daughters, your menservants and maidservants, and the Levites, the aliens, the fatherless and the widows who live in your towns. For seven days celebrate the Feast to the Lord your God at the place the Lord will choose. For the Lord your God will bless you in all your harvest and in all the work of your hands, and your joy will be complete. Three times a year all your men must appear before the Lord your God at the place He will choose: at the Feast of Unleavened Bread, the Feast of Weeks and the Feast of Tabernacles. No man should appear before the Lord empty-handed: Each of you must bring a gift in proportion to the way the Lord your God has blessed you."

Deuteronomy 16:1-17

HOLY DAYS AND HOLIDAYS
IN THE GOOD LIFE

9 Holy days . . . holidays. There is an obvious connection. I've thought a lot about the connection
between holy days and holidays and I wondered if
given the way that holy days started out, and the way that
holidays have developed, there might not be a parable here of
the way that we look at the things of God. Of course, we can
go a step further. Holy days became holidays which became
vacations. A vacation is a time to vacate. To vacate means to
make vacant. It means to empty out. It means, as the young
people put it, to "veg." We've come a long way haven't we,
from holy days to "vegging." In actual fact, holy days were full
and vegging days are empty. I wonder if in the move from holy
day to holiday to vacation we might not have a picture of the
drift to secularism in our society.

God's Instructions for Holy Days
God gave some general instructions about Feast Days or Holy
Days and then He gave some quite specific instructions. In
Leviticus 23, we have a more detailed account of the feasts
than in Deuteronomy 16. "The Lord said to Moses, 'Speak to
the Israelites and say to them: "These are My appointed

feasts, the appointed feasts of the Lord, which you are to proclaim as sacred assemblies" ' " (23:1-2). Notice that certain feasts and festivals were appointed by the Lord and were to be regarded as sacred assemblies. The two expressions, "sacred assemblies" and "appointed feasts," suggest to us that God was very serious about instituting certain things into the lifestyles of His people for very specific reasons. The term "appointed feasts" reminds us that He appointed a specific place where the feast should be held. Over and over again God insisted that they were to attend the place He would choose. They couldn't engage in these festivals anywhere they wished — it was an appointed feast at an appointed place. Neither could they do it any time. Over and over again He gave meticulous instructions as to the exact timing of these festivals. In addition He gave detailed instructions concerning what they were to do when they got there. Appointed procedures, place, and time, all designated by the Lord. Clearly, there was a time set apart for the purpose that He had in mind. God knows how forgetful we are; unless He stipulates specific things, we will probably forget all about doing what He asks us to do. We manage to forget, even when He has stipulated His expectations in great detail.

The Sabbath Day was one of the festivals to be observed on a weekly basis. A lot of people think that the Sabbath concept began with the Ten Commandments. In actual fact, the idea of the Sabbath predates the Ten Commandments by a long, long time. In the account of God creating the world, we are told He worked six days and on the seventh day He rested. There is the first indication of one day in seven being set apart.

When the Children of Israel were in the wilderness, they grumbled and growled because they didn't have the food they enjoyed in Egypt, but they overlooked the fact that God managed to feed them miraculously with the manna. They never did figure out the manna, but called it "What is it?" They didn't like it and grumbled about that as well. But He kept providing it morning by morning. Actually, He didn't provide it every morning, because one day it didn't show up—the seventh morning. They were told to collect the right amount each day; if they collected too much it would stink and rot, and all their neighbors would smell their greed. If they didn't collect enough, they would go hungry. But on the sixth day God sent an extra amount and they were allowed to collect a double supply, because on the seventh day they were not to do any work. God was building the Sabbath into the structure of their lives. On a weekly basis there would be one day specifically set aside for sacred assembly, when the people would take time to rest, reflect, and to be refreshed. That is a principle that God built in right from the time of the Creation.

There are two expressions related to the Sabbath Day that we should remember. One is that it is "blessed" by God. That means it came from God as a benediction, as a gift, as an expression of concern by God to His people. And not just to His people either, but also to His animals. The Children of Israel were instructed to give their beasts of burden one day off in seven. In other words, they treated their animals better than some people today treat their employees. Not only that, the Sabbath was declared to be "holy." That meant that God claimed it as His special day. God's reasonable expectation was that on at least one day in seven, people would recognize that He had a claim on their lives and would put other things to one side and come before Him for rest and refreshment and spiritual renewal.

Three specific festivals or feast days are mentioned in Deuteronomy 16. Now there were many others that you can read about in Leviticus 23. These three, the Feast of Unleavened Bread, the Feast of Weeks, and the Feast of Tabernacles are specifically mentioned, however, because it was mandated that the men should attend. They had to go to the place of God's choosing and present themselves before the Lord. This meant that there was an element of pilgrimage about it, because the place that God established was Jerusalem. Three times a year, therefore, the men, specifically, had to make sure that they stopped what they were doing, left their homes, made the pilgrimage to Jerusalem, and engaged in the holy days. It should be interesting to us in our society, where more women tend to worship than men, that we should recognize that it was the men who were given the responsibility for pilgrimage.

● Let me just briefly sketch for you these three specific festivals. The first one was the *Passover*, closely related to the Feast of Unleavened Bread. When the Children of Israel were in Egypt, they were suffering terribly at the hands of their taskmasters. God determined to deliver them and sent His servant Moses to confront Pharaoh. Pharaoh was immensely powerful and he needed the Children of Israel for slave labor, and so he wasn't about to let them go. There were various confrontations and in the end God said that unless Pharaoh let His people go, He would bring judgment to bear upon them in that the firstborn of each family would die. He told the Children of Israel that they should take a year-old lamb, a male without blemish, and sacrifice it on a certain evening; they should splash the blood on the doorposts of their homes and then they should eat the meat together. The whole point of the blood being sprinkled on the doorposts was that when the Angel of Destruction saw it, he would pass over those families and they would be saved. In addition, they were to be ready to flee from Egypt. They would not have time to bake their bread, to put in the yeast to let it rise normally, so they were to simply bake some bread without yeast (unleavened bread), grab it and get out of there as soon as the judgment fell. Hence, the Feast of Unleavened Bread.

God intended the monumental events of the redemption from Egypt and the Exodus out of Pharaoh's control to be constantly remembered by people. The only reason they could enter the good life was that God had intervened in their affairs, redeemed them, and given them the land of promise. Therefore, they were to go to Jerusalem every year and reenact the Passover for seven days, eating unleavened bread in order that they would never, ever forget the Passover and the Exodus.

● Then there was the annual *Feast of Weeks*. The end of the Feast of Passover was the beginning of harvest. As soon as they got into their harvest, they were to take the very first sheaf of corn or grain and present it to the Lord; hence, the expression "firstfruits." By bringing the firstfruits they were actually saying, "We fully recognize, Lord, that You deserve the credit for our harvest and, therefore, right off the top we bring to You our expression of thanksgiving." Seven weeks after bringing the firstfruits, they were to celebrate the Feast of Weeks at the end of harvest.

When I first started preaching in England in little churches in the country areas, one of the great ecclesiastical events was the annual harvest festival. On that day the church would be decorated with produce from the farms round about, all kinds of grain in big beautiful golden sheaves, all kinds of vegetables, and fruit. Everyone brought something to remind us that without God's gracious provision we wouldn't have a thing. The old farmers would squeeze themselves into their one Sunday suit, looking terribly uncomfortable because they hadn't worn it since the previous harvest festival, and with their big old horny hands clutching hymnbooks, they would sing the wonderful old hymns of thanksgiving and praise. The Feast of Weeks was something like that. It was a remembrance that if it hadn't been for the Covenant God choosing them as His people, giving them the land, overwhelming their enemies, and giving them their corn and sending the rain and sunshine, they wouldn't have survived. So the Feast of Weeks was a remembrance of the harvest. It was the recollection of their utter dependence upon God and they were grateful. And God said, "Be there!"

● But then there was the third main pilgrimage feast — the *Feast of Tabernacles.* Passover was the end of March or the beginning of April. The Feast of Weeks was the end of May or the beginning of June. The Feast of Tabernacles was late September or early October. On this occasion they would chop down branches from the trees and make them into little huts, and during the Feast of Tabernacles, they had to live in these rather uncomfortable surroundings. It can get pretty chilly in Israel in October. They had left their homes, trekked all the way up to God's appointed place, made their little tabernacles and there they were. Why did God tell them to do this? Because forty years while they wandered in the wilderness without any permanent home, God had provided for them, had protected them, had cared for them and had worked out His purposes through them. But once they got into their comfortable homes, they could easily forget how He had cared for them. So God prescribed an annual camping trip in the Fall so that they would never forget what He had done for them in the wilderness. "Be there," He told the men.

● So we see the specific instructions that God gave concerning holy days. We have identified the weekly Sabbath and the annual festivals but there was also a monthly commitment that they were required to fulfill, the Festival of the New Moon. This did not mean that they worshipped the moon. They were agriculturalists, so they were very much tied into natural phenomena; every time they saw the new moon they realized that the Covenant God had graciously brought them through another month. Therefore, on a monthly basis they would bring their expressions of thanksgiving to Him. Weekly Sabbath, Monthly New Moon, Annual Holy Days — these were built into their lifestyle.

God's Intentions for Holy Days

Now let us think about the divine intentions concerning these holy days. It is one thing to receive God's instructions, but we need also to understand His intentions. Why was God insisting that the people of God in the Promised Land go through all these rituals? I've come to the conclusion that there were three things God had in mind.

● He was concerned about the need for His people to *congregate,* hence the expression "sacred assembly." To assemble or to congregate means to bring people together. God stipulated that His people should come together on a weekly, monthly, and annual basis. Why was this? The more prosperous we become, the more independent we are. The more independent we are, the more isolated we live, unless we carefully craft into our lives a willingness to subject our individualism to a concern for corporate living. There is an individualistic streak in all of us, a tendency to isolation. The more self-sufficient we become, the less inclined we are to commit to community affairs. But that is a very dangerous thing for the people of God. In fact, it's a dangerous thing for anybody. So God carefully crafted into the lifestyle of these people the absolute necessity to congregate together in assembly before the Lord. We need to reiterate this to God's people today. Right from the beginning of time, God has made it abundantly clear that He expects His people to have specific times put aside for rest and refreshment and renewal and reflection as they congregate on a regular basis. "Be there," He says! I'm afraid we have become very casual in this area.

I remember with great gratitude my parents teaching me that wherever I was on the Lord's Day, I should be in a place of worship if at all possible. I'm grateful that this principle was built in from my earliest days, and I can testify to the fact that there have been relatively few occasions when the Lord's Day has not found me with His people.

It's interesting to notice how seriously this was taken by the Lord Himself. He travelled up to Jerusalem regularly for the Feast Days, and it was His custom to be in the synagogue on the Sabbath Day. The Apostle Paul was particularly anxious on one of his missionary journeys to make sure he was back in Jerusalem for the Feast Day. The people wanted him to stay, but he insisted he had to get back there. On the Day of Pentecost, the people who responded to Peter's sermons came from all over the world. Why? Because they understood they should be there at Jerusalem on the Feast Day. There was an intention on God's part to bring together people in congregations, and it is imperative that the Lord's people today remember that this is a fundamental of the good life.

• There is the need not only to congregate but also to *celebrate.* They celebrated the Feast of Tabernacles and the Feast of Weeks. When we talk about celebration, we're talking of great joy. A lot of people don't like congregating with God's people because they think it is so dull and so drab. They are more interested in having fun. "Fun" is a key word in our society today. I'm not suggesting that worship should be fun, but I am saying that true worship is celebration! It is an expression of rejoicing and of joy.

Sarah was very much concerned when she was an old lady that she didn't have any children. Her husband who was older was even more concerned, and then God, in a wonderful way, provided a son for them, and Sarah was just tickled to death about the whole thing. She laughed when she first heard she was going to have a baby—and did she laugh when the baby was born! That was why they called him Isaac, which means "laughter." Sarah said, "God has brought me laughter and everyone who hears about this will laugh with me."

Did you ever think of God bringing you laughter? Did you ever think of God bringing you joy? Did you ever think about God being a God of rejoicing who brings you so much joy and so much laughter and so much exhilaration into your life that when people get around you they laugh, they rejoice, they are exhilarated too? You see, that's the point of bringing God's people together—to celebrate. We need that if we are to live the good life.

Singing played a major role in the celebrations. When Jerusalem became the appointed place of worship, the pilgrims came from their home up to Jerusalem (they said "up to Jerusalem" because it was a higher altitude than the rest of the country). As they came up to Jerusalem they sang all the way. Great crowds of people marching along singing their hearts out, climbing the hill all the way! That's why their songs — Psalms 120-134 — were called the Songs of Ascent.

Singing together, lifting their spirits together, praising the Lord . . . one of the best cures for depression is praise. One of the best cures for discouragment is thanksgiving. One of the best cures for loneliness is congregating. God knows we need it, and so He built in the holy days. And He said, "You will be there to celebrate. You will be there to congregate."

There was an emphasis on sharing as well. "No man should appear before the Lord empty-handed: Each of you must bring a gift in proportion to the way the Lord your God has blessed you" (Deuteronomy 16:16-17). That is the favorite verse of every church treasurer, and what an important point it is. Part and parcel of the celebrating, the joy, and the singing is the sheer joy of giving. When you enjoy giving unto the Lord, what you are really saying is, "Lord, You are so good and You are so great and You are so gracious; here is an expression of my gratitude. But I have to admit that I'm dependent on You even for expressions of gratitude. But that's how it is and I love You." What a wonderful thing to meet on a regular basis, not empty-handed, but singing your heart out, laughing your head off, celebrating, congregating. That was His intent.

• Then there is the need to *concentrate*. God's people have a need to congregate. They have a need to celebrate. They have a need to concentrate. If we don't recognize that God has built in times for physical rest, we probably won't take them. I have failed in my life in this regard, and I'm trying to make some adjustments right now. If we do not recognize the need for carefully crafted times of spiritual renewal, when we concentrate not only on the ceremony, not only on the activity, but also on the practical details of our life, it is possible that we will drift through life without seriously coming to grips with what it is all about. When the people went up to Jerusalem for the Passover, it was very difficult for them to go through the motions without thinking of the immensity of God's intervention. As they celebrated the Feast of Tabernacles, it was very difficult for them to go through the motions and forget the intensity of God's care for His people in the wilderness. God instituted certain rites in their lifestyles in order that they might get the proper physical rest, might have careful spiritual refreshment and renewal and then build into their lives the practical realities of their utter dependence upon the God who provides all things. Life is so filled with trivia that care must be taken to concentrate on matters of substance. God planned specific days to help make this happen.

God's Irritation Concerning Holy Days

God gave His ancient people some specific instruction concerning holy days; but slowly and surely, the holy days became holidays. The significance seeped out and people began to use them for their own purposes, rather than for the purposes for which they were ordained. Hence the divine irritation concerning holy days. One of the key emphases of the prophets was to express divine dissatisfaction with the abuse of the holy days by God's people. There were times when they simply, flatly ignored them altogether. Whole generations went by and the Feast of Tabernacles wasn't celebrated once. In fact, generations were born and they didn't even know about it. The whole thing fell into total disregard. Then there were times when they went through all the motions of the festivals but stripped them of significance, and this was deeply irritating to God. Speaking through the Prophet Amos, God made the remarkable statement, "I hate, I despise your religious feasts . . . Away with the noise of your songs!" (Amos 5:21-23) "I hate them," He said, "and I'm tired of all your singing." Why? Because they had stripped the form of its reality. They were making of it what they wanted for themselves, and refusing to see the significance.

Another thing that irritates God about the way people handle His holy days is when they are observed with reluctance. In Amos' time some of the people were saying, "How quick can we get this New Moon celebration over so we can open the shops again?" Other people were saying, "These Sabbaths are a nuisance—they are interfering with what we really want to do."

The question may come to your mind, "Are we supposed to be celebrating these feasts now?" Some of you might be thinking, "I wouldn't mind a trip to Jerusalem three times a year, if someone paid for it. I'm not too excited about staying in little booths in bad weather, but there's a Hilton on the Mount of Olives, isn't there?" The New Testament teaches that all the feast days, all the festivals, were a shadow, but that the substance is Christ. God's people are supposed to recognize in Christ the substance which all these festivals foreshadowed. (See Colossians 2:16-17.)

The Lord's Day is the day I set aside time for rest, to remember the creation, to remember redemption, to worship, to celebrate, to congregate; to make absolutely certain that there is a time in my life for Christ to be the unshaken, unmoving focal point of my day.

What about the Passover? Passover became Easter, and we have Easter full of eggs and bunnies. But if Passover became Easter and Passover prefigures Christ in His death and His resurrection, and if unleavened bread speaks of Exodus and Exodus reminds us of Christ's Exodus from the grave, what in the world are we doing with Easter bunnies and eggs, when the substance is Christ?

What about the glorious feast of the Incarnation? The won-

131

derful reminder that Word became flesh, dwelt among us, full of grace and truth. But now we've got Santa Claus! What in the world are we doing? We have become utterly secularized, we have become desperately commercialized; we maintain the shadow, but the substance is Christ.

I wonder if an evidence of our secularization is the move from holy day to holiday to vacation. I wonder if the time has come for those of us who want to enjoy the good life, God's way, simply to say, "Lord, thank You for the opportunity to congregate with Your people and celebrate with Your people and concentrate with Your people. And thank You for the unspeakable privilege of building this into my lifestyle weekly, monthly, annually so that whatever else happens, I never lose sight of the fact that the substance of my life is Christ. I'm sorry I got so mixed up with all kinds of other stuff and missed the point."

When you have entered the land the Lord your God is giving you as an inheritance and have taken possession of it and settled in it, take some of the firstfruits of all that you produce from the soil of the land the Lord your God is giving you and put them in a basket. Then go to the place the Lord your God will choose as a dwelling for His Name and say to the priest in office at the time, 'I declare today to the Lord your God that I have come to the land the Lord swore to our forefathers to give us.' The priest shall take the basket from your hands and set it down in front of the altar of the Lord your God. Then you shall declare before the Lord your God: 'My father was a wandering Aramean, and he went down into Egypt with a few people and lived there and became a great nation, powerful and numerous. But the Egyptians mistreated us and made us suffer, putting us to hard labor. Then we cried out to the Lord, the God of our fathers, and the Lord heard our voice and saw our misery, toil and oppression. So the Lord brought us out of Egypt with a mighty hand and an outstretched arm, with great terror and with miraculous signs and wonders. He brought us to this place and gave us this land, a land flowing with milk and honey; and now I bring the firstfruits of the soil that You, O Lord, have given me.' Place the basket before the Lord your God and bow down before Him. And you and the Levites and the aliens among you shall rejoice in all the good things the Lord your God has given to you and your household.

"When you have finished setting aside a tenth of all your produce in the third year, the year of the tithe, you shall give it to the Levite, the alien, the fatherless and the widow, so that they may eat in your towns and be satisfied. Then say to the Lord your God: 'I have removed from my house the sacred portion and have given it to the Levite, the alien, the fatherless and the widow, according to all You commanded. I have not turned aside from Your commands nor have I forgotten any of them. I have not eaten any of the sacred portion while I was in mourning, nor have I removed any of it while I was unclean, nor have I offered any of it to the dead. I have obeyed the Lord my God; I have done everything You commanded me. Look down from heaven, Your holy dwelling place, and bless Your people Israel and the land You have given us as You promised on oath to our forefathers, a land flowing with milk and honey.' "

Deuteronomy 26:1-15

THE PLACE OF WORSHIP
IN THE GOOD LIFE

10 In England if you address a mayor, you call him "Your Worship." This does not mean that all British politicians are particularly religious. In fact, it has absolutely nothing to do with religion. What it means is that mayors, because of their position, are regarded as people who have worth. Because they have worth they are worthy of respect—hence, worship. Worth, worthy, worship. To worship somebody means, literally, to attribute worth to them, to give them the respect they deserve. When God commands His people to worship Him, He is really making absolutely certain that they render to Him that which is His due. The Hebrew word for "worship" is translated in verse 10 by the English words "bow down." In both the Old Testament and the New Testament, the idea of worship incorporates the sense of "bowing down." The Book of Deuteronomy relates how on numerous occasions the people of Israel were given instructions as to whom they were *not* to worship, where they were *not* to worship, how they were *not* to worship. But there were specific, positive instructions too. So *worship* could have positive or negative connotations, depending entirely on who or what was being bowed down to. It was assumed that people living in the good land would understand the place of worshiping the Lord.

Now it used to bother me very much that God seemed to want people to worship Him. I had the impression that God was on some sort of divine ego trip, sitting up there requiring everybody to stand in line and worship Him. It bothered me more that that was my perception of God, but it bothered me most that I even thought like that. Then one day I discovered that C.S. Lewis had the identical problem, and I found, at last, that I had something in common with C.S. Lewis! He said he got the idea that God was saying, in effect, "What I most want is to be told that I'm good and great." The mental image that I had was of God sitting on His big throne, waiting for people to file past Him and say, "God, You're good and You're great," and He would beam with appreciation! Lewis helped me, because he not only articulated his problem but also came up with an answer:

> I had never noticed that all enjoyment spontaneously overflows into praise. . . . The world rings with praise. . . . I had not noticed either that just as men spontaneously praise whatever they value, so they spontaneously urge us to join them in praising it. . . . Therefore praise not merely expresses, but completes the enjoyment. In commanding us to glorify Him or worship Him, God is inviting us to enjoy Him.[8]

If you enjoy something, part of the enjoyment is talking about it. How many men watch a football game, and then relive the event by talking about it? Their enjoyment of the game is intensified by the spontaneous act of sharing the enjoyment. That's why God wants us to worship Him. He has created deep within us a sense of His worth, but to express it with other people serves only to intensify and enrich the enjoyment. Hence, God requires us to worship Him, not for His benefit, but for our own. In this passage there are at least three ways in which worship may be expressed.

Worship Makes a Statement

To worship is to make a statement. The Israelites were told that at the time of harvest they were to gather the first fruits of the harvest, put them in a basket, take them to the place of worship, present them to the priest and then to say certain, prescribed things. They were to make specific statements.

● The first was a statement of *appropriation*. They were to say, "I declare today to the Lord your God that I have come to the land the Lord swore to our fathers to give us." (26:3). In other words, they were saying, "Lord, You promised this good and pleasant land to Your people, but a lot of them never made it here. I did, and I stand before You now testifying that I have appropriated the blessings that You have made available to me."

This is the essence of spiritual life and worship. God makes blessings available to us, but we come into the good of them only when we appropriate them to ourselves. This is true in every dimension of our lives. God gives us air, but does not breathe it for us. God provides food for us, but insists that we eat it ourselves. He graciously gives us clothing but never, ever dresses us. He provides the blessings and we appropriate them. In exactly the same way, the land promised to the Children of Israel was theirs for the taking, but they had to appropriate it and possess it. A worshiper is somebody who is making a statement to the effect that they are living in the glad appropriation of what God has made available to them.

● The second was a statement of *appreciation*. The people were required to recite, "My father was a wandering Aramean, and he went down into Egypt with a few people and lived there and became a great nation, powerful and numerous" (26:5). They were saying that they were very conscious of their *spiritual heritage* and wanted to express appreciation for it.

When I worship I appreciate all that has gone into making it possible for me to be a worshiper. I appreciate the place provided by those who have gone before. My mind roams back over the years rejoicing in a godly heritage.

Some of us can look back one generation, two generations, three generations, to godly people whose lives and testimonies form a train of blessing. Others of us say, "I come from a dysfunctional family; I'd give my eye-teeth to be able to artic- ulate appreciation for my spiritual heritage, but I don't have one." Well you may not be able to see it in your immediate family, but you can certainly see it in your culture. You can certainly see the heritage in your country, your denomination, your church or parachurch organization. We are all spiritually rich in heritage, and when we present ourselves in worship we acknowledge our deep appreciation for those who have gone before.

But we also express appreciation for *personal redemption*. The prescribed statement went on, "But the Egyptians mistreated us, and made us suffer, putting us to hard labor. Then we cried out to the Lord. . . . the Lord brought us out of Egypt with a mighty hand and an outstretched arm . . . He brought us to this place" (26:6-9). This was a recital of the redemp- tion they had experienced because of divine intervention. When I worship I articulate deep appreciation for my own personal redemption. In the same way that the Israelites re- counted their appreciation of the Exodus out of Egypt, so I rejoice in a personal redemption I enjoy because Christ has broken the bondage of sin in my life and set me free to live and serve Him in newness of life. When I come to worship, I express deep appreciation for the fact that Christ has inter- vened in my life, in times when I was living in bondage to fear, depression, discouragement, and all kinds of sin. Because Christ moved in through the work of His cross and the minis- try of His Spirit, I may sing with tremendous enthusiasm. Or, I may participate in a liturgical service and recite the Apostles'

Creed and sing the Te Deum. Or, I may join in a contemporary worship experience where hands clap, feet stomp, and arms are raised in praise.

Then we express appreciation for *temporal blessings.* The statement goes on to say, "For the Lord brought us out with a mighty hand. . . . He brought us to this place and gave us this land, a land flowing with milk and honey" (26:8-9). When we recognize that all we have materially and temporally, we have because of God's gracious concern for us, it is only right and proper that we should make a top priority of expressing our appreciation to Him. We should thank God for all that sits in our kitchens, garages, and bank balances. So we put all this together and we see that an integral part of worship is to make a statement concerning what we appropriate and what we appreciate.

● The third was a statement of *adoration.* "You and the Levites and the aliens among you shall rejoice in all the good things the Lord your God has given to you" (v. 11). There is to be a sense of delight, a sense of joy, a sense of cheerfulness, a sense of adoration, when we come before the Lord in worship. I fully recognize that there are different styles of worship. Some people feel that it should be conducted in a very orderly, solemn manner. They like to worship in a place that looks like a church, where there are liturgy and vestments, and symbols to help us remember that God is high, holy, and awesome, and that we come into His presence with tremendous reverence. And there is no question in my mind that this is a perfectly legitimate kind of worship. On the other hand, we can sometimes become so set in our ways, so rigid in our approach, that we lose all sense of freedom and joy. That is why in many churches freedom is the key word. We find people enjoying services where they can clap their hands and jump up and down in the aisles, shout "amen" and "hallelujah," exercise their spiritual gifts, and generally have a good time. Who is to say that there is not an appropriateness to this aspect of worship too? The form is not the important thing. What is important is that our hearts are lifted up in ecstatic adoration of the Lord, because having focused on Him, our understanding of Him has led us to attribute worth to Him. For He alone is worthy!

• The fourth was a statement of *anticipation.* The required statement ends with a plea to the Lord, "Look down from heaven, Your holy dwelling place, and bless Your people Israel" (26:15). Here the worshipers are looking up to heaven in great need, conscious that God is looking down in all His gracious power. As they bring their needs to Him, they do so in keen anticipation that He who has promised to meet all their needs will do so. Not necessarily their wants, certainly not their whims or caprices, but definitely their needs. So to worship is to come before Him making a statement, "Lord, here I am. I've appropriated what You've given me, I appreciate all that You have done, I adore You because You are worthy, and I want You to know that I anticipate that You will continue in the future to be the faithful God You have proved to be in the past." That is worship.

Worship Makes a Sacrifice

To worship is to make a sacrifice. The instructions concerning worship were straightforward. At the beginning of harvest, the farmer was to leave his fields, go to the place of worship, and present the basket of firstfruits there. Just imagine that you are that farmer. Your crops are ready for harvesting, it is a critical period, your year's work will be finalized in the next few weeks. You've got to get to it, but as soon as you have reaped the first little bit you have to stop, leave your farm, and truck all the way to Jerusalem. Would you be too enthusiastic about that? But this is what God told them to do!

• They were required to make a sacrifice of *time.* They were not free to simply fit worship around their busy schedules. *They were to build their busy schedules around the priority of*

140

worship! That called for sacrifice. Not infrequently today we find that people will worship if it is convenient. Their lives are full of all kinds of activities and they are very happy to worship, provided it does not intrude on the things they really want to do. I can assure you that the farmers in Israel really wanted to get their harvest in, but God said, "Leave it. Now is the time for worship."

When I was growing up in England I saw farmers who would not touch their harvest on the Lord's Day, even though it had rained all week and the forecast was that it would rain all next week and the only sunny day was Sunday. But they left it in the field and it sometimes cost them their harvest, but they had a very simple basic principle: "We will express our appreciation of the Lord at the appropriate time, and that's a priority."

● I want you to notice also that leaving their harvest and going all the way to the appointed place of worship meant a sacrifice of *energy.* They were going to have to get themselves to the place God had determined. Travel in the Holy Land in those days was not easy. It's not easy today either. It's very hot at times and it's very cold at other times. The terrain is rugged, and it's very exhausting, even traveling around in an air-conditioned tourist bus. In those days, to travel on foot or by donkey on those dusty, barren paths was very taxing, but they were required to do it. That meant a sacrifice of their energy, which was part of their worship.

One day David wanted to build a temple for the Lord. He knew exactly the piece of property he wanted for the site—a threshing floor. He went to the man who owned it and made an offer. When the man realized why David wanted the property he said, "If that's what you want it for, I'll give it you." And David came out with a great line, "Shall I offer to the Lord that which costs me nothing?" He said it in such a tone of voice that the answer was obviously, "No way." He thought, "If I am going to truly worship the Lord, there must be an element of sacrifice involved. If I really believe that He is worthy of my praise, He is worthy of sacrifice on my part."

• Then there was a sacrifice in terms of *property*. The procedures for worship are meticulously recorded in Deuteronomy 26. You can read more about them in Deuteronomy 12 and, of course, in Exodus and Leviticus. The worshipers were required to bring at different times and occasions "burnt offerings," "sacrifices," "tithes," "special gifts," "vows," "free will offerings," and "firstfruits." This meant that if they were to worship in the structure God had ordained, it was going to require a considerable sacrifice, not only of time and energy, but also of property.

Included in that list is the little word "tithe." Now that's a word that strikes fear in many a believer's heart today. The idea of giving a tenth of your income to the Lord is terrifying and horrifying. We know this to be the case, when we look at the percentage of giving that is common in the church in America today. The average is much nearer 3 percent than 10 percent. I want you to notice something important. Tithing was just *one* aspect of their giving. Tithing or a tenth of their income was given off the top to the Lord, and then after that there were burnt offerings, sacrifices, special gifts, free will offerings and firstfruit offerings. Ten percent was just the base; then they started giving. In other words, in those days, to worship not only meant a sacrifice of time and energy but of property too. Why? They knew if the Lord had not put them in that land, they would have nothing to live on. If the Lord had not helped them survive in the wilderness, they would not have been living anywhere! If they had remained in Egypt, they would still be in a real pickle. It was only because of the Lord that they had what they had and were where they were.

Worshipers today need to realize that they are in a similar position; they demonstrate appreciation in carefully prepared and executed worship, which includes sacrificial giving.

Worship Expresses Submission

To worship is to express submission. At the beginning of the chapter, I pointed out that the Hebrew word for worship means "to bow down." In the New Testament one of the Greek words for worship literally means to "bow down and kiss." Both words contain the same idea of "submission to an authority" or "worship." Hence, to worship is to bow down before the Lord and make a statement, make a sacrifice, and express submission.

When we truly worship the Lord, we bring ourselves in our entirety before Him, and submit ourselves in our entirety. As we discover more of Him, we become caught up in who He is and we are wonderfully delivered from that wretched self-centeredness which Archbishop Temple says is our "original sin and the source of all actual sin." How significant it is that we should learn to truly worship in submission before Him!

• Now let me suggest to you some specific ways in which this works. Worship should be an *intellectual exercise.* I must bring my mind to church in order that it might grapple with the immense truths of God. A lot of people have the idea that worship is simply something you do by physically putting yourself in a pew, or it is something emotional which generates a warm fuzzy feeling. No, worship has to start out with me bringing my mind to bear upon God's revealed truth, so that the Holy Spirit can begin to speak to me as I open and submit my mind to the truth revealed. I should, therefore, be carefully prepared for worship. If I come to worship with my mind filled with all kinds of other things, it's quite possible that I will be three-fourths of the way through the worship hour before I can even start concentrating.

Jill and I have to drive half an hour to our church, and in that time we have the opportunity to quietly prepare our hearts and our minds for worship. We pray together, we quietly meditate, or one of us will read to the other the Scriptures for the day. Preparation is taking place so that when we arrive at the place of worship our minds are already on track.

● Worship is an *emotional exercise.* As our minds begin to grapple with truths that are deeply moving, tears may be appropriate. If the truths are exhilarating, laughter might be spontaneous. If the things that are being discovered speak peace to the heart, a tremendous sense of well-being results; and if there is a confrontation with the awesomeness and the holiness of God, a deep sense of holy fear may develop.

● Then, of course, there is the will, for worship is a *volitional exercise.* It is perfectly possible for minds and emotions to be geared into the truth, but for there to be no worship. For to truly worship is to submit my will to the things God is saying. For instance, if I come into church from a life of sin, and I listen to the Word, make confessions of the Creed, sing the songs and I go out straight back to my old sin, I may have attended a worship service; but in the truest sense of the word I haven't worshiped!

It is rather unfortunate that the English language has one word for worship and another for service. In many other languages only one word is necessary; this is helpful because it emphasizes the fact that when I come before the Lord, bringing all my abilities to bear upon Him in worship, the natural overflow of the exercise is a life of service.

Let me suggest two things to you. First, if we, as the church, really learn to worship, fund-raising will no longer be necessary. I firmly believe that. If we come sacrificially before the Lord with our tithes and our offerings, we won't have to be fiddling around with budgets, starting out with what we ought to do, paring it down to what we think we can do, cutting back to what we think may be possible to do and then slicing off another 20 percent because we have got to think realistically about what the people will give!

Second, a truly worshiping community wouldn't need recruiting drives. Our problem would be finding enough tasks for everybody to do, rather than finding enough people to do what is necessary to keep the doors open and the wheels turning. Our delightful problem would be finding the appropriate places in which to channel the offerings and the tithes of God's people.

At the end of every seven years you must cancel debts. This is how it is to be done: Every creditor shall cancel the loan he has made to his fellow Israelite. He shall not require payment from his fellow Israelite or brother, because the Lord's time for canceling debts has been proclaimed. You may require payment from a foreigner, but you must cancel any debt your brother owes you. However, there should be no poor among you, for in the land the Lord your God is giving you to possess as your inheritance, He will richly bless you, if only you fully obey the Lord your God and are careful to follow all these commands I am giving you today. For the Lord your God will bless you as He has promised, and you will lend to many nations but will borrow from none. You will rule over many nations but none will rule over you.

"If there is a poor man among your brothers in any of the towns of the land that the Lord your God is giving you, do not be hardhearted or tightfisted toward your poor brother. Rather be openhanded and freely lend him whatever he needs. Be careful not to harbor this wicked thought: 'The seventh year, the year for canceling debts is near,' so that you do not show ill will toward your needy brother and give him nothing. He may then appeal to the Lord against you, and you will be found guilty of sin. Give generously to him and do so without a grudging heart; then because of this the Lord your God will bless you in all your work and in everything you put your hand to. There will always be poor people in the land. Therefore I command you to be openhanded toward your brothers and toward the poor and needy in your land."

Deuteronomy 15:1-11

PROSPERITY AND POVERTY AND THE GOOD LIFE

11 When I arrived as the new pastor of Elmbrook Church, many people came to tell me how excited they were about Elmbrook and how nervous they were that I might ruin it. They told me about the good things that were happening and obviously wanted me to make sure they continued. One gentleman said that one of the great things about Elmbrook Church was that they never mentioned money. He added, "We have all come from churches that talk about money all the time." I said to him, "I thought they taught the Bible at Elmbrook Church." He said, "They do. They just don't get involved in all this money stuff. They just teach the Bible."

I pointed out to him that the Bible says an awful lot about money, and I had a problem if I was to teach the Bible but never to mention money. Now this was only his perception. My predecessor did teach the Word of God and certainly did not evade the issues the Bible presented.

There is a certain skittishness in some people on the subject of money, particularly as it relates to spiritual life. Yet the simple fact of the matter is that one of the most accurate gauges of spirituality is the way we handle our material resources. Our spiritual life is lived out in a material environment, for that's the only arena we have to live in.

Now when the Lord began to talk to the people of Israel about going into the Promised Land and enjoying the good life, He was clearly promising that they would prosper materially, and that it was important for them to understand how to handle this prosperity appropriately. I'm sure they were very interested in the subject because they spent a considerable amount of time in abject poverty in the wilderness. The idea of trading their poverty for relative prosperity must have been very attractive indeed, and they were undoubtedly ready to enjoy the good life, particularly as it related to material prosperity. Deuteronomy 15 is about prosperity, but it is also about poverty. It is the balancing of these two things that we need to consider if we too are to enjoy the good life, because our attitudes toward poverty and prosperity are part of properly enjoying the good life.

The Promise of Prosperity

First of all, notice the promise of prosperity. There is no question that the Lord was promising to richly bless them in the land. He told them that the land was their inheritance, and He was giving it to them. This, of course, was all part of the covenant. In exactly the same way that Moses was pointing back to the deliverance that God has given to them, he was pointing forward to the inheritance that God would give to them. As surely as deliverance was theirs, the inheritance would be theirs, and the inheritance included the good land, and the good land included material prosperity.

● The promise of prosperity had a *cooperative aspect to it*. On the one hand, God promised, "I will richly bless you." On the other hand, "If you fully obey." I will—you do. That's cooperative. He promised, "I will give the land," but added, "You must go in and possess it." The land was there, but it was populated by a number of tribal groups that needed to be driven out. They would be driven out because, "I will fight for you." They were going to do the fighting in His strength. "I will richly bless"—you must obey. "I will give you the land" —you must possess the inheritance.

The same principle applied when God reminded them that when they got into the Promised Land and began to prosper materially, there would be the tendency for them to say to themselves, "My power and the strength of my hands have produced this wealth for me." But He said, "Remember the Lord your God—it is He who gives you the ability to produce wealth and so confirms His covenant." Why were they going to prosper materially? Because God had put it in His covenant and because He gives the ability to get wealth. If they simply sat there and said, "We have prospered because we have worked hard, and we deserve it, and it's all the result of who we are," God would say, "No, it isn't, it's a result of My covenant, and it is a result of My giving you the ability to get wealth." However, having admitted that they would still have to exercise their God-given abilities, the blood and the sweat and the tears would be theirs. They were going to have to work hard to prosper materially in the land. The promise was based on the covenant which assumed a cooperative effort. They were going to fulfill their responsibilities and God was going to be faithful, and they must never emphasize one at the expense of the other.

I like the story of the pastor who was visiting the farmer. They walked around the farm and then went into the farmhouse for a cup of coffee. Sitting by the window looking out over the farmland the pastor said, "You know, it's a wonderful farm the Lord has given you here. Just look at what He has done. Look at those rolling hills, those lines of corn, the beautiful rows of produce." The old farmer listened and then said, "You're absolutely right. He has given me a wonderful, wonderful place and you should have seen the mess it was in when He had it on His own!" The old farmer made a good point. When the Lord has a farm on His own, it does tend to be a bit of a tangle, and that's why He looks around for people who will cooperate with Him, so they can get things sorted out.

But what is more important is that we should listen to God leaning out of heaven saying, "You should see a farm that man has on his own. No soil, sunshine, or rain. No miracle of reproduction and no seed." If anybody dares to suggest that we can produce wealth either all on our own or all because of God, they are not thinking straight. It is covenant based, but it is also cooperative. God will richly bless, but we've got to obey. He will give the land, we've got to possess it. He gives the ability to get wealth, we've got to use our ability.

● Then there was the *corporate* aspect. You'll notice that God was not so much interested in individual prosperity. He was talking about a land, a nation, the people of God, and the Children of Israel. This comes through very powerfully in verse 6: "The Lord your God will bless you as He promised, and you will lend to many nations but will borrow from none." Notice that this was not going to be a nation that would run on a deficit. Also, "You will rule over many nations, but none will rule over you." God was not talking about individuals here, but about society, about the community, and about the nation as a whole. It is not that God was disinterested in individual prosperity, but rather, as far as His people were concerned, He was thinking about national and societal prosperity. Why is that? Because the land that He was making available to His covenant people was for all of them, not just a few, and He was particularly concerned that it be available so that all of them could live in the good of it.

Principles for Today

The question that we now need to address is how far is this applicable for us today. For example, is the Industrialized West the Promised Land? Are sophisticated, technological

Westerners the covenant people? Do the principles that God outlined for Israel obtain today? More than 300 years ago a group of people sailed out of England and came to America believing that it was the Promised Land and they were the covenant people. They were getting away from Europe and they were going to America to establish a city set on a hill. There was an element of truth in what they had to say, but clearly America is not the Promised Land and North Americans are not the covenant people. Nevertheless, there are principles here that certainly apply to the people of the new covenant, the Christian church. What are these principles?

● "The earth is the Lord's." As soon as a Christian says this, he finds himself in major disagreement with both the capitalists and the communists. For the capitalist says, "The earth is ours," and the communist says, "The earth is the state's," but the Christian says, "The earth is the Lord's." The capitalist says, "The resources that I have, I got through the sweat of my brow and they are mine." The communist says, "The resources we have are available to the state for the common good." But the Christian says, "The resources that are available to mankind belong to the Lord."

● Not only is the earth the Lord's and the fullness thereof, but mankind has been placed on earth as manager of God's resources. As manager, he is to cooperate with God. There is no way that man can handle resources that are divine without divine initiative and divine intervention, but clearly man has responsibilities; therefore, there is a cooperative system. The earth is the Lord's, man is the manager of the Lord's resources, and man is to cooperate with God.

● In addition God encourages man as manager by saying, "As you manage My resources well, I will allow you the privilege of enjoying the products of your labor. You will prosper, but remember they are My resources, and you're managing them for Me. As you have the privilege of enjoying the products of your labor, managing My resources, remember that I require you to dispense some of the resources you're enjoying to further My concerns for the whole of mankind. You will dispense My resources at My instruction."

The Problem of Poverty

Now we turn our attention to the problem of poverty. There are some people who love to find "contradictions" in the Bible. I'm always happy to help them look and then discuss them. In verse 4 we read, "However, there should be no poor among you." Then notice in verse 11, "There will always be poor people in the land." It's really not a very difficult problem, because the first is an idealistic statement and the second is a realistic appraisal. The idealistic statement is, "There should be no poverty whatsoever among you." But the realistic appraisal is, "There will be." Now why is this the case?

It is interesting to notice that there are at least nine different Hebrew words translated "poor" or "poverty" in the Old Testament. There appear to be three kinds of poverty God is concerned about. The first is what we call *economic* poverty. That is where people are deprived of life's basic necessities. The second is *political* poverty—that is, where people are deprived of justice and freedom. And the third kind of poverty is *spiritual* and *emotional,* where people are deprived of hope and consolation.

God said that when His people moved into the Promised Land, they were to expect that there should not be any economic, political, spiritual, or emotional deprivation. Why? Not because all the causes of these things had been eradicated, but because the resources to counter them would be there in profusion. In other words, God was saying, "I will richly bless you and if you utilize what I'm making available to you, there should be no poverty in the land." That is a profound statement. The big thing, of course, is that society must respond to God's Word and do things God's way. That's where we move from the idealistic statement to the realistic appraisal.

Unfortunately, the realistic appraisal is that there will be poverty in the land for one simple reason. It is not that God has failed, not that the resources are not available, but that man has not handled divine resources properly. Therein lies the problem. We need to recognize how true this is. For instance, if you look at the international scene at the present time, you will see there is an inequitable distribution of material resources. Now if the earth is the Lord's and the fullness thereof, and it all belongs to Him, and mankind in general is managing it, why then is there such an inequitable distribution of the world's resources? The World Bank reported, "Approximately twenty percent of the world's population continues to be trapped in absolute poverty. A condition of life so characterized by malnutrition, illiteracy, disease, squalid surroundings, high infant mortality and low life expectancy has to be beneath any reasonable definition of decency." John Perkins has said that poverty is much more than lack of money — that poverty is lack of options. When people are economically deprived, they are deprived in every dimension of their lives. Twenty percent of the world's population live in that abject condition.

John Stott has pointed out that the wealthy nations of the world spend twenty-one times the amount of money on armaments that they spend on development for poor nations. For every $1 million that wealthy nations make available to deal with abject poverty, they spend $21 million on armaments. This is obscene.

Let's look at the church of Jesus Christ. Is there a linkage between the church of Jesus Christ in the affluent West and the impoverished rest of the world? Well, if we're all acknowledging Christ Jesus, clearly there is. Then what should we be thinking about the material resources that we have in relative abundance, as opposed to the lack of fundamental resources in the impoverished rest of the world? This is difficult for some of us to address because we have never known anything other

153

than the church in the West. I was in a pastors' conference in Zambia many years ago, and realized that there was some degree of tension among the Zambian pastors. I asked a missionary who had lived there all of his life, "What's the problem?" "Oh," he said, "it's the old, old problem that some of these pastors are quite well-to-do and others aren't doing very well at all, and there is some jealousy between them." I said, "I'm sorry to hear that but I don't see much sign of affluence around here." We were meeting in a place with no walls, there was frost on the ground, the only heating and lighting we had came from burning cow dung, and we were sitting on logs on the earth floor! He said, "Well, haven't you seen their bicycles?" I said, "What do you mean?" He said, "Some of these pastors have bicycles. They are the affluent ones who come from the wealthy churches. They were able to get here in one day's ride on the bicycle and the others had to walk for five days. That's where the tension comes from." The Zambian pastors were so poor that to own a bicycle was to be affluent — and to be envied! The problem for many Western Christians is that they don't know how wealthy they are because they have never seen how poor the rest of the world is. But when we recognize world poverty and Western affluence, we are then required to sacrificially give to those who are equally members of the human race and should be sharing God's good earth and its benefits.

As we look at this problem of poverty we say to ourselves, "Why is it here?" There are two reasons that I want to identify. Clearly some people live in poverty because they have made some bad choices, and they are living with the consequences. But if we simply assume that everybody who is impoverished or deprived is living with the consequences of their own wrongdoing we are quite wrong. Many are in poverty because they have sinned, but many live in a deprived condition because they have been sinned against. What comes through very clearly in Deuteronomy 15 is that often the "sinning against" is from the hand of those who prosper, because when the request comes for aid, the response is "hard-hearted," "tightfisted," and "evil-eyed"—the literal expression of "wicked thought." Evil-eyed means that we look with cynicism and skepticism, with hard, harsh, cold calculating snake eyes, and do nothing about the poor. This is the problem of poverty.

The Practice of Generosity

Mandated in this passage of Scripture is what I will call the practice of generosity. God has given a very simple principle: "There should be no poor among you. I'm going to richly bless you. You've got to go in there and thoroughly enjoy everything I'm giving you, but you have a responsibility to care for those who are not as fortunate in the community. You fulfill this responsibility by generosity."

Now notice some of the procedures that were required. For instance, verse 1, "At the end of every seven years you must cancel debts." Now I have lost all my banker friends! In verse 8, "Be openhanded and freely lend whatever he needs." The expression *freely lend* means "interest free loans." Now I've lost my investment counselor friends! If you lent somebody something, they repaid it in a responsible way. But, if at the end of six years, they couldn't repay it all, you said, "Okay, forget it." Also, it was an interest-free loan! This is how the people were to live in the Promised Land—mandated generosity.

Some people who went to the ultimate in impoverishment and deprivation would sell themselves into slavery. But after six years they must be released. And notice how they were to be released: "When you release him do not send him away empty-handed. Supply him liberally" (15:13-14). I hear people sometimes talking with great concern about liberals. *Liberal* is a wonderful word. Listen, "Supply him liberally from your flock, your threshing floor and your wine press. Give to him as the Lord your God has blessed you." This was required of the people living in the Promised Land. Sure, they were going to prosper, certainly they were going to have an abundance. They were going to administer it as they enjoyed it, and they were going to cancel debts on the seventh year, and they were going to give interest-free loans, and when slaves were liberated they were going to heap them up with all kinds of things.

And, on top of that, they would give their annual tithe! Now a *tithe* is another word for 10 percent. They were required to take 10 percent of all their produce and hand it over to the Lord's representatives who would administer it for the work of the Lord and for the care of those who were deprived.

Then there were what they called the gleaning rules. When they harvested, they weren't to pick up every little grain. In fact, if they forgot a sheath they weren't to go back and get it. They were to shake the trees to get the fruit off, but the fruit that didn't come off they were to leave. The reason was very simple: the deprived people could then come behind and glean. It wasn't a welfare handout that was going to exacerbate poverty and increase dependency. The poor people would have to work, but the prosperous people made these things available to them. Isn't it interesting that God had promised prosperity, wanted to eradicate poverty, and gave these generosity principles to His people?

Principles for Today
The only question that remains now is how much of this applies today? Well, you must work out the details for yourself, but there are some principles here that apply. We know this because they make their way all through the New Testament. Study the church in Jerusalem, study the churches that Paul established in Macedonia and Achaia and the regions beyond. Read James' instructions to the church in Jerusalem, and then note the letter that Jesus dictated to the church in Laodicea. There are certain principles that find their way from

the Old Testament into the New Testament and right down through the ages.

First, God's people are to give *generously*. That is one of the characteristics of God's people, they give generously. Second, they do it *without grudging*. Third, they do it *in proportion* to the way that God has given to them. Because of this the Lord promises to bless them even more abundantly. Now you'll find all that in verses 10-14.

Let me suggest some very simple things for our own giving, our own generosity attitude.

• Our giving should be *rational*. It is relatively easy to become very emotional about giving. Emotional as to the reason why I shouldn't or emotional in the way that I do. There are plenty of people in the Christian community today who know how emotional people are in their giving, and they know exactly how to play on those emotions. A lot of Christian giving is purely emotional, impulse giving. It is not careful, rational giving at all. This is what I mean by careful, rational giving: If I know, for example, that 10 percent of my income is not mine, but the Lord's, then I don't need to get emotional about that. I just need to get very rational and get out my pocket calculator in case I can't divide by ten and figure out what that amount is, right off the top. I don't touch it, because it is there to give away. That's a good way to start.

• Now, of course, some of us will find that 10 percent of nothing much amounts to nothing much, but we give it ungrudgingly and live on the balance. But some of us will discover that 10 percent of a lot is a lot! And with the 90 percent that is left, we just buy more and more stuff that we don't need while lots and lots of people don't have what they do need. Is that how it should be? No! We don't stay with 10 percent, but we then give offerings. So everybody participates, but the principle here is that the giving is *proportional*. God always works on the principle that people should give in proportion to the way that He has blessed them.

● Then we give in a way that is *sacrificial*. If we are to bring our tithes and our offerings, there is always a sense of sacrifice involved. As I prepared this study, I reviewed our giving for the previous year and this was the question I asked myself, "What have I done without the previous year because I gave the money away instead?" Now the extent to which I can answer that question will determine the extent of my sacrificial giving. Giving should be rational, ungrudging, proportional, and sacrificial. It should be done on the basis of God's covenant and my stewardship. It's all His and I manage it.

Now what I am commanding you today is not too difficult for you or beyond your reach. It is not up in heaven, so that you have to ask, 'Who will ascend into heaven to get it and proclaim it to us so we may obey it?' Nor is it beyond the sea, so that you have to ask, 'Who will cross the sea to get it and proclaim it to us so we may obey it?' No, the word is very near you; it is in your mouth and in your heart so you may obey it.

"See, I set before you today life and prosperity, death and destruction. For I command you today to love the Lord your God, to walk in His ways, and to keep His commands, decrees and laws; then you will live and increase, and the Lord your God will bless you in the land you are entering to possess.

"But if your heart turns away and you are not obedient, and if you are drawn away to bow down to other gods and worship them, I declare to you this day that you will certainly be destroyed. You will not live long in the land you are crossing the Jordan to enter and possess.

"This day I call heaven and earth as witnesses against you that I have set before you life and death, blessings and curses. Now choose life, so that you and your children may live and that you may love the Lord your God, listen to His voice, and hold fast to Him. For the Lord is your life, and He will give you many years in the land He swore to give to your fathers, Abraham, Isaac and Jacob."

Deuteronomy 30:11-20

DECISION-MAKING
FOR THE GOOD LIFE

12 Moses was told by the Lord that while the Children of Israel would be allowed to go into the Promised Land, he would not. He would be permitted to go on to the top of Mount Nebo and look down into the valley and see this gorgeous land, but he would be denied entry. One of the most poignant moments of my many trips to the Middle East came when I stood on Mount Nebo on the point where Moses had stood with all the wilderness behind him and the magnificent vista of Israel before him. It was not difficult to get some sense of what must have been going through Moses' mind, as he stood there and then turned to the people of Israel and reminded them that they had a big decision to make. What were they going to do about what God had said to them, bearing in mind that their parents had had a similar decision to make forty years earlier, and had decided in the wrong. As a result they had wandered forty years in the wilderness.

With tremendous concern, Moses saïd to them,

Now what I am commanding you today is not too difficult for you or beyond your reach. It is not up in heaven, so that you have to ask, "Who will ascend into heaven to get it and proclaim it to us so we may obey it?" Nor is it beyond the sea, so that you have to ask, "Who will cross the sea to get it and proclaim it to us so we may obey it?" No, the word is very near you; it is in your mouth and in your heart so you may obey it. See, I set before you today life and prosperity, death and destruction. For I command you today to love the Lord your God, to walk in His ways, and to keep His commands, decrees and laws; then you will live and increase and the Lord your God will bless you in the land you are entering to possess. But if your heart turns away and you are not obedient, and if you are drawn away to bow down to other gods and worship them, I declare to you this day that you will certainly be destroyed. You will not live long in the land you are crossing the Jordan to enter and possess.

This day I call heaven and earth as witnesses against you that I have set before you life and death, blessings and curses. Now choose life, so that you and your children may live and that you may love the Lord your God, listen to His voice, and hold fast to Him. For the Lord is your life, and He will give you many years in the land He swore to give to your fathers, Abraham, Isaac and Jacob.

Life is made up of decisions. Of that we are all very much aware, but we're not always aware of the magnitude of the decisions we make at the moment we make them.

The mayor of Pittsburgh and his wife were leaving a hotel on one occasion, having been to a certain event, and they walked past a building site. One of the laborers on the building site, when he saw the mayor's wife, waved to her and called her by her first name. To the surprise of the mayor his wife waved back and he turned to her and said,

"Do you know him?"

She said, "Yes, I dated him before I met you."

He said, "You dated him?"

She said, "Yes, I did."

He said, "Do you realize that if you would have married him you would be the wife of a laborer?"

She said, "Yes, and do you realize that if he had married me, he might be the mayor of Pittsburgh?" Decisions!

An eleven-year-old girl was reading a book with her English governess. The book contained all the names of the kings and queens of England and the girl was fascinated. The governess turned to her and said, "One day your name will be on the bottom of this list." The little girl burst into tears at the thought of that awesome responsibility. Then she stopped crying, wiped her eyes, stood up and said, "I will be good." At the age of eleven, that little girl called Victoria made a decision that altered the course of the British Empire, and the world.

A young boy was listening to a sermon on the grace of God. At the end of the sermon an offering was received. The usher came up to the little boy, who asked, "Would you lower the plate please?" So he lowered it, but the boy said, "Lower." The boy kept asking for the plate to be lowered until finally he said, "Put it on the floor." The usher, wondering what was in the little boy's mind, put the offering plate on the floor and the little boy jumped up from his seat and stood on the offering plate. William Carey, the father of modern missions, was the little boy who offered himself that day. The face of India and the world was changed.

Life is made of decisions. That's why we need to be very careful to make the right ones. Of course, some decisions are made for us.

John and Greg Rice are twins. They are also dwarfs who stand slightly less than three feet tall. When their mother saw them, she abandoned them at birth. They were dealt a poor hand in the game of life, but they made a decision. They decided that they were going to play the hand anyway. When they grew up, they went into business selling real estate in Florida and became millionaires. So many people attracted by their success came to these twin dwarfs and asked how they had done it, the twins found that they were spending more time explaining their success than working. So they sold their real estate business and started giving seminars entitled, "Think Big." Imagine going to a seminar with twin dwarfs teaching you how to think big! The result is that hundreds of thousands of people have responded as John and Greg Rice have challenged them to refuse to regard themselves as victims and to make positive decisions which will change their lives.

Life is full of decisions. Some are made for you, but most you make yourself. Some you realize at the time are going to be profoundly significant. I was not asked if I would like to be born British—no one consulted me. If they had, of course, I would have said, "Yes, please!" I did, however, decide to become a banker. I did decide to join the Marines. I did decide to marry Jill. I did decide to leave banking and go into the ministry. I did decide to leave England and move to America. That is what my life is all about—decisions.

Moses, addressing the Children of Israel, said, "Now you've got a big decision ahead of you. I've told you about the covenant of God, I've told you about the initiatives that He has taken. I've told you about the land that He will give you. I have reminded you of the Exodus. I have reminded you of what He has done for us in the wilderness. I have reminded you of the fact that He promises to fight for you, and I have reminded you that life is going to be full. It's a good life if you live it God's way. Now then, you make the decision! Are you going to do it His way? Or are you going to do it your own way, like your fathers did. Let me remind you, if you do it His way, the blessings of the good life are yours. If you do it your own way, you'll live with the consequences." There was no confusion in the minds of those people. They understood the options and the consequences.

Decision-Making and Freedom

In our modern age, of course, we get very philosophical about decision-making. We've got all kinds of theories about human freedom and our ability to make decisions. There are the determinists who say that man is not really free to make a decision. He is the product of all that has made him the person that he is. Therefore, his decisions were really pre-empted by the determining factors of his life.

The naturalistic determinists say your environment or your genes have made you the person that you are. The family that you were born into, the climate, the sociological structures are all decided for you and you are simply the product of all these determining naturalistic elements. While there is no doubt a considerable amount of truth in this theorizing, Scripture doesn't allow us to be naturalistic determinists because it tells us that we are able to make decisions, that we are responsible to do so, and that we will live with the consequences of our decisions.

Then there are the *theistic determinisits.* They say that our lives are determined by God—that the sovereign God predestines and because He predestines we simply fit into all that He has predetermined for our lives. While Scripture clearly teaches the sovereignty of God, it also teaches human responsibility. Any approach that denies human choice and human responsibility tends to dehumanize human beings and must be resisted.

There are also *indeterminists.* They believe that events do not have a cause—things just happen. The national anthem of the indeterminists is "Que sera sera." There is no rhyme or reason to life. There is no order, no cause, no effect. Life just goes along. So jump aboard and enjoy the ride as long as you can. This notion denies divine purpose in our lives, and must be rejected.

Then there are the *self-determinists.* They are really saying, "It's up to you, mister—you're out there in a big cold world and it's entirely up to you to make out of your life whatever you can. Nobody else is going to help you—you've got to look out for Number One. Get out there and hack out your own life. Nobody else can be counted on—just you—don't worry about God, He is probably not around. If He is, He is so old He is out of it, so it is entirely up to you. You determine your own life."

Divine Sovereignty and Human Responsibility

What do we make of these philosophical approaches? Well, of course, we put them under the search light of Scripture. As we do this we discover two interesting things. Scripture clearly teaches divine sovereignty and it clearly teaches human responsibility, and theologians have been trying to put the two together ever since they started reading the Bible. Divine sovereignty says that God is in control—that all things come from Him, exist for Him, and ultimately are accountable to Him. But the Bible also teaches that whilst God is sovereignly in control, man under His sovereignty has the responsibility and the ability to choose and is required to make good decisions in line with the sovereign will.

Genesis 2 explains this very nicely. It describes how our original parents were put in a beautiful place to live. God walked them around the garden, showed them all the fruits and the vegetables that were growing there and said, "Enjoy, just enjoy." Then He added, "By the way, you see that particular tree there? Don't touch it!" So the sovereign Lord outlined what He had in mind for them. He had sovereignly decided to create them. He had sovereignly decided to put them in the Garden, give them all manner of food to eat, and He had sovereignly decided that they were not to touch one particular area, and He had sovereignly decided they were perfectly free to choose anything else within His sovereign limits. They were not expected to come to God every day asking about the menu. They were a big boy and a big girl.

They made their own decisions, but they were predicated on what God's initiative had determined for them. So we see the divine sovereignty right from the very beginning, outlining the limits of human freedom within which human beings are free to choose.

When the Prophet Ezekiel was around, there was a very popular proverb, "The fathers have eaten the sour grapes and the children's teeth are set on edge." God didn't like that proverb and He forbade them to use it anymore. You say, "What's wrong with that proverb?" Well, the proverb really meant something like this, "Hey man, the reason that I am the way that am with my teeth set on edge—has absolutely nothing to do with me. It's my old man's fault. He ate sour grapes and I am the unfortunate product of a sour-grape father. So is it any surprise that my teeth are constantly set on edge? I am the adult child of a sour-grape-eater." God said, "Don't use that anymore, because every man is accountable for his own sin" (Ezekiel 18:2-3).

While we do recognize that environment and genetic make-up, the family, and many other factors affect us, making us the people that we are, we also have to accept, on the basis of Scripture, that we do not have the freedom to push the responsibility for our lives on somebody else. Life has dealt us a hand of cards. There is no question about that, but we are required to play the hand we have been dealt, to make the right decisions, and to live with the consequences.

Let me illustrate it for you. Friday night I'd like to invite you all to come out to dinner to our home in Oconomowoc at 7:00 P.M. We'll have steak. That's my decision. I've decided to invite you. You don't have to come but you are perfectly free to come. You say, "I think I'd rather come on Thursday— I've got a date on Friday." I didn't invite you on Thursday. You say, "I don't want to come on Friday." You're perfectly free not to come. Your choice is not going to affect my choice. It is not going to change, but it doesn't change the fact that you are free to choose. Somebody else says, "I was brought up a strict Catholic. Can we have fish, not steak?" I say, "No. It's going to be steak—that is my decision. I fully understand that your family background has certainly affected the way you live, but the decision is entirely yours." Somebody else says, "My parents aren't very happy with me mixing with evangelical Christians like you, particularly with beards, and if I come then I could upset my parents. I have a conflict because I would really like to come but I do want to keep things good with my parents." That's going to affect your decision as well, but it is still your decision. So you've got my invitation—my choice is Friday night and steak. You don't have the freedom to come on Friday for fish or on Thursday for steak. But you are free to come or not to come on Friday for steak.

Decision-Making and Facts

Now, of course, decisions are often made on impulse. Those of you who shop in supermarkets know this to be true. I'm told that you should never shop in a supermarket when you are hungry, without a list, and you should never shop with somebody else. The reason for all this is that people who run supermarkets have found the most delightful, beautiful ways of getting you to part with your money painlessly. A lot of it on impulse. That is why there are always long lines at the checkout counter so that you stand in line against all the magazines and the candies. The kids are going to yell and scream for candy and you will leaf through the magazines and buy both. Impulse buying! Impulse decisions are very similar and are often wrong decisions. As we say in England, "Marry in haste and repent at leisure."

Moses was not asking the Children of Israel to make an impulse decision. He was asking them to make decisions based on solid information. He also insisted that the decision was "not too difficult for you and not beyond your reach." It was not hidden, shrouded in the mists of heaven so that somebody would need to go up there and figure it out and come back. Neither was it beyond their reach as if it was over the sea and an expedition would need to go out, explore it, and return. In actual fact it was already in their hearts and in their mouths which meant they had already heard it, already assimilated it, and already gotten the facts. They had been talking and discussing the issues one to the other so the problem was not understanding it, the problem was deciding what they were going to do.

Now at that point probably some of the Children of Israel said, "Moses, could you just refresh our memories about the nature of this decision?" He said, "Yes, I'll tell you very simply what it is. The Lord is your life. Therefore, choose life. That's it, the Lord is your life, therefore choose life." Somebody may have queried, "What's the alternative?" Well, it would be that I decided the Lord is not my life and, therefore, I will choose to live my own life. Now it's hard to imagine how it could be much simpler than that. Either the Lord is the Lord of life and I choose to acknowledge Him as the Lord of my life, or I decide the Lord is not the Lord of life and I choose not to acknowledge Him as the Lord of my life! That is not too difficult. It is not beyond anyone's reach. The decision is already in your heart and in your mouth. You've heard it, you've understood it, you've talked about it, you've discussed it, you've argued, you've debated. Now decide! William Barclay put it this way, "Many a man's refusal of Christ comes not because Christ puzzles and baffles his intellect, but because Christ challenges and condemns his life."

I was talking to a university student in England years ago. He had all kinds of intellectual questions, and I did the best I could to answer him. In the end I said, "Look, you've asked me many questions. May I ask you one question?" He said, "Sure." I said, "Just supposing I can answer all your intellectual questions so that you come to the point of being absolutely convinced that Jesus Christ is the Lord of life. Would you then become a dedicated, devoted disciple of Jesus Christ?" "No, I wouldn't," he replied. I said, "Then you are a phoney, because you've kept me here for an hour pretending you've got intellectual problems when, in actual fact, you've got a moral problem."

So Moses said, "Now you've got the good land ahead of you, you've got the good life ahead of you. The good Lord is there, and He wants you to acknowledge His Lordship and live in obedience and dependence upon Him. Choose!" To help them in this decision Moses also outlined the options for them. He said, "I have set them before you very clearly and I call upon heaven and earth as my witnesses, the unchanging heavens and the unchanging earth that have seen it all, and therefore, in the context of history understand what I am saying to be true. I have set before you life and death, blessing and cursing. Choose!"

The options are very clear. You remember the suzerainty treaties, that the big king would make with the little king? Toward the end of those treaties there appeared a list of the blessings that the little kings would enjoy if they acknowledged the big king. And in small print there was a list of the penalties they would incur if they didn't acknowledge the big king. Allan Bloom in his book *The Closing of the American Mind* said, "America today has no-fault insurance and no-fault divorces, and it is moving with the aid of modern philosophy toward no-fault choices." In the divine economy we will never, ever, be given no-fault choices. There will always be blessings or cursings. There will always be things that accrue to our benefit and there will also be penalties dependent upon the choices that we make. We would like to have the total freedom to decide as we will and have absolute sovereign control of the consequences of our decisions, but that freedom is not ours. Life and death, blessing and cursing. God's way or your way. Life or not life are the options. Choose life!

What did Moses mean when he said, "The Lord is our life

and we should choose life"? All physical life originates in the Lord. When He becomes the Lord of our life, then our physical existence is invested with eternal significance and we know why we are here. Spiritual life is also found in Him. A great gulf has developed between the God from whom we come and to whom we go and ourselves. We come from Him and we go to Him, and in the interim we are supposed to live by Him. But we've lost Him.

Christ is the Lord of life in the sense that He has bridged the gulf and makes it possible for us to be reconciled to God and hence begin to be tuned into Him. That is the essence of spiritual life. He is the One who, having died and risen again, has moved into the presence of God and has opened a way into His presence for all eternity and offers us eternal life through His Spirit. He is the Lord of physical existence and He is the Lord of spiritual reality. He is the Lord of eternal assurance — life. And we can choose to respond to Him or we can choose to reject Him. The decision is all ours. We can either come before Him in humble dependence or we can stand against Him in arrogant independence. Humble dependence says, "I do not have the ability to be what I am created to be. I need the gracious ministry of a loving God in my life. I have tried to do it my own way — it has not worked, I have not been the person I ought to be. When I examine my heart I find shame and guilt. I haven't even been what I myself profess to be, let alone what I'm called and created to be. I come humbly before God and I confess my need. I'm rejecting this arrogant independence of God that suggests that I can do it myself and I'll come seeking His grace and mercy." I can choose between loving obedience or willful disobedience — that's the choice. Moses said, "Choose life that you may live."

Decision-Making and Follow-up

Now, of course, we're well aware of the fact that decisions can be made in a knee-jerk fashion. Sometimes people are manipulated into decisions. The tragedy, however, is that so often this type of decision has not resulted in a newness of life. The real decision, the real commitment to the Lord of life, however, has a follow-up built into it. Notice how Moses puts it, in the second half of verse 19, "Now choose life so that you and your children may live and that you may love the Lord and listen to His voice." Did you notice the words *Live, Love, Listen?* Moses obviously learned to preach in England — three points all beginning with *L!* If you choose to acknowledge the Lord of your life, it is going to affect you for the rest of your days. It isn't just a snap decision that says, "Yes, I have not lived a very good life and, O God, I'm sorry and, O God, forgive me." And then go straight out and live the same old life. No, this is a decision to acknowledge the Lord of life, fully understanding that He will change the direction of your life en route to life eternal. You will be so taken by the love of the Lord in making this available to you that your heart will be stirred with love for Him. This will become the motivating factor of your life. Up till this point in life there have been all kinds of other motivations and all kinds of other mechanizations. But now because you acknowledge the Lord of your life and His love to you, you find kindled within you a love for Him and that love for Him is going to be demonstrated by a genuine desire to please Him.

It also means that on a regular basis you will listen to Him. You will not order your life on the latest craze of secularized society. You will order your life by listening to what He has said on the basis of eternal truth, and you will make decisions for your life based on loving Him and listening to Him. The Children of Israel had the great advantage of having it all explained to them and Moses concluded by saying, "I call heaven and earth as witnesses against you that I have set before you life and death and blessings and cursings. Now choose life."

May I urge you to choose and enjoy the good life.

ENDNOTES

1. James Reichley, *Religion in American Public Life*, Washington, D.C.: The Brookings Institute, 1985, 344.
2. Ibid., 11.
3. C.S. Lewis, *The Problem of Pain*, New York: Macmillan Publishing Company, 1962, 150–51.
4. Arlene S. Skolnick and Jerome H. Skolnick, *Family in Transition*, Boston: Little, Brown and Company, 1986, 532.
5. Charles Swindoll, *Growing Wise in Family Life*, Portland, Oregon: Multnomah Press, 1988, 32.
6. Paul Vitz, *Psychology as Religion: The Cult of Self-Worship*, Grand Rapids: Wm. B. Eerdmans Publishing Company, 1977, 91.
7. Ibid., 141.
8. C.S. Lewis, *Reflections on the Psalms*, New York: Fontana, 1961, 80.